# Be successful; be spiritual!

## How to serve God in the workplace

'Everyone…will find valuable
biblical guidance in this book.'
—Jerry Bridges, Author,
*The Pursuit of Holiness*

**John Temple**

DayOne

© Day One Publications 2008

First printed 2008

ISBN 978–1–84625–109–2

British Library Cataloguing in Publication Data available

Published by Day One Publications

Ryelands Road, Leominster, HR6 8NZ

☎ 01568 613 740 FAX 01568 611 473

email—sales@dayone.co.uk

web site—www.dayone.co.uk

North American—e-mail—sales@dayonebookstore.com

North American—web site—www.dayonebookstore.com

Cover design by Wayne McMaster

Printed by Gutenberg Press, Malta

*Be successful; be spiritual!* is a thorough study of the biblical principles underlying all of work and business. Everyone, from the person just entering the work force to the experienced CEO, will find valuable biblical guidance in this book.

**—Dr Jerry Bridges, Author, The Pursuit of Holiness**

*This book will show countless people that true success has a sound spiritual basis, and I warmly commend it.*

**—Dr John Blanchard, internationally-known author, evangelist and conference speaker**

# Contents

# Contents

# Contents

# Contents

# Contents

# Contents

# Contents

*Dedication*

To all my colleagues, past and present, as an apology for the many occasions

that I failed to live up to the standards that I set out in this book.

# Author's note

My work experience has been in international business, working in Africa, Australia, South East Asia, Britain and the USA. I have also done extensive business in Europe. All of the illustrations quoted are true, although they may have been simplified and modified in such a way as to avoid embarrassment to the parties involved. The examples are similarly true or reconstructed from situations based on my personal experience. Examples will, therefore, be in various currencies. As far as possible, I have tried to include advice for all of the countries with which I am familiar.

# Acknowledgements

The writing of this book came about as a result of encouragement from Brian Edwards. I thank him for his practical help in initiating the project and also for reading an early version of the manuscript—no doubt, a trying experience! I also appreciate him making his lecture notes on leadership available to me.

Over many years, I grappled with the consequences of progressing in a secular career (if there is such a thing) while having, at the same time, the desire to live as closely as I could to God's standards. Many people helped me in my thinking, notably Professor Jan van Rooyen, a former professor of law at the University of South Africa. Colleagues, too numerous to mention, also drew my attention to my many failings and suggested appropriate remedies. As always, my wife and, later my children, would raise issues which sharpened my thinking. I appreciate them all.

I wish to express my appreciation to Dr John Blanchard for writing the Foreword and for his invaluable editorial comments; my thanks, too, to Dr Jerry Bridges for his endorsement. Both of these men have also indirectly contributed to this book through the instruction that I have received by reading their books and in many private discussions with them. Thanks are due to Dr Eric Hayward for checking chapter 5 and to Andy Benfold for checking chapter 1.

I am grateful to Mrs Sue Holmes for editing the entire book and to my wife, Yvonne, and my granddaughter, Rachel van der Merwe, who helped to remove errors and improve my grammar.

I am also grateful for the many other books which have contributed to my thinking. Some of these I have listed in the reference section. I have also suggested further reading material in 'Endnotes'.

Finally, I would be nowhere without God's revelation to us all, namely, the Bible. This is the only safe guide and I have tried to be faithful to it. Any errors or misguided views are my own.

My prayer for this book is that it may enlighten and encourage all Christians to work in a manner which makes them successful and, at the same time, brings glory to God.

**John Temple**
Burley, England, 2008

The Christian community has long lacked a book that gets to ruthlessly practical grips with issues that occupy most people in the developed world for two-thirds of their waking hours—working, earning money and the management of their resources, whether these are large or small. Ideally, such a book should be written by someone who has begun 'in the trenches', worked and studied hard, and risen to the top of his profession, yet never lost sight of the fact that his primary call in life was to honour God by his obedience to biblical principles.

This is it.

John Temple began his working life by (literally) getting his hands dirty and learning his trade the hard way, constantly learning from those around him and gradually honing his natural gifts by adding to his formal education. This twin-track approach paved the way for significant progress in his chosen profession, eventually propelling him to positions of significant influence and authority. These experiences lie behind the pages that follow.

Beginning with a Christian view of economics, he tackles difficult subjects such as leadership, management of people, the responsibilities of employers and employees and the maintenance of rigorous integrity in a valueless postmodern world. He laces his teaching with vivid case studies, illustrating how it plays out in practice and at every point shows how clear biblical principles point the way to true success as opposed to the mere accumulation of wealth.

Choosing a pension, the 'dos and don'ts' of investing and the right use of one's so-called 'retirement years' are all handled with obvious expertise and with refreshingly frank references to his own experiences in these areas.

This book will show countless people that true success has a sound spiritual basis, and I warmly commend it.

**John Blanchard**

Whe I left school, I was convinced that, as a Christian keen to evangelize, I should become a pastor or some other 'full-time' Christian worker. So, I registered at university to study history (my favourite subject) with the intent of studying theology later. Somehow, this did not really fit my self-perception and so before the academic year began, I switched to Engineering. However, the desire to serve God 'more fully' (as I saw it then) never left me and so fifteen years later, I found myself in secular employment and an elder in a church that I had helped to found. One Sunday I had preached my heart out and was standing at the door to greet the congregation as they left when a relatively new member stopped at the door and initiated a conversation which went something like this: 'John, you are a businessman, are you not? You know how to make money.' I was a bit taken aback as this is not the usual farewell from a member of the congregation, so I probably nodded something in the affirmative. 'Well, then,' he continued, 'why not concentrate on being a really good businessman, make a lot of money and then hire someone who can really preach?' I knew that he had trained for the so-called full-time ministry but had himself followed precisely his own advice, so I was not at all offended. It was a watershed in my thinking. Although I had not thought through my views on work at that time, I slowly realized that 'full-time service' included my secular job as much as anything else. I took his advice and, while I still preach occasionally, I prefer to sponsor others more gifted at it. My secular job became my calling and I set out to do it as well as I knew how. In time, it yielded financial fruits but this was not what I was pursuing.

The message of this book is to show that God intends us all to work and that there is no divide between so-called secular employment and 'full-time Christian service'. Both are important in God's economy and we can, and should, glorify him in both. We glorify God most when we point men and women to the cross, which means seeing our jobs as a mission field.

Most adults will spend two-thirds of their waking lives at work. In all probability, their jobs will be the source of their financial support and, perhaps, even define who they think they are. In most western cultures, roughly half of us will be employed in government or by some impersonal corporation. The other half will be self-employed, in professional practice, in a church or mission, a non-profit organization or a small 'friends and family' business. Some will be at the start of their careers, perhaps in their first job, while others will be at the top in positions of leadership. Still others will be on pension. This book is for all of you.

Is this book for men only? Not at all. The instruction to work is given to both men and women. The work of many women will be as homemakers but, while this is a great and noble job, I shall not be dealing specifically with it in this book. Perhaps, some women will go beyond being homemakers. In which case, they may find this book even more useful.

What is 'work'? In this book, we shall be dealing mainly with that component of work which brings in our living. However, work has a much wider meaning. John Stott[1] defined it as 'the expenditure of energy (manual or mental or both) in the service of others, which brings fulfilment to the worker, benefit to the community and glory to God'. I would broaden that slightly to include the earning of a living. It includes all that we do around our homes, assisting others and so forth. Put differently, it really includes much of what we do every day, except for recreation and leisure. A key element of work is the concept of service. This book is, therefore, for men and women who seek to glorify God by following his revealed plans for work. It is not about poverty eradication even though the Bible does teach that 'a slack hand causes poverty, but the hand of the diligent makes rich' (Proverbs 10:4). Consequently, we shall touch on poverty because its cure is to get men and women to work. For a more detailed analysis of work (and leisure), I recommend Leland Ryken's scholarly work *Work and Leisure in Christian Perspective*.[2]

I have tried to make the principles of the book applicable to all forms of work. Inevitably, my perspective in the *applications* is governed by my own experience which, though wide and varied, nevertheless covers only a small spectrum of disciplines. It may help you to know my background. My early postgraduate career was as a research engineer or scientist. I progressed to engineering management and then into business management before becoming chief executive or chairman of a number of companies in South Africa, Australia, South East Asia, the UK and the USA. In parallel, I lectured at two universities in the UK and three in South Africa. I have been on the governing councils of educational institutions, ranging from a nursery school to a university. At the same time, I became a property developer, designing and building domestic residences. Also, in parallel, I was active in founding churches and have held virtually every office of leadership within a church. Through all of this time, I sought to understand the principles of working as God intended us to.

Wherever we find ourselves, it will be assumed by our employers that we know how to behave in our culture, i.e. we will 'default' into certain patterns of behaviour which are the product of our assumptions about our fellow human beings, relationships, the economy, leadership, wealth and so forth. We will also be the product of our education and training. This is known as our *world view* or 'cosmological beliefs'.

As Christians, we all too easily slip into the prevailing world view. This may be true even if we are slightly troubled as to how to reconcile our beliefs with the prevailing secular world view. We may notice a difference between what we learn on Sundays or in our Bible studies and what is assumed in our secular jobs. One common way of dealing with this dichotomy in our beliefs is to compartmentalize our lives into a 'spiritual component' for Sundays and a 'secular component' for the working week. This is known as 'dualism'. Is this correct? (See Alistair Mackenzie and Wayne Kirkland, *Where's God on Monday?* for a full debate on this issue.[3])

It may even be worse than that. Sometimes, we are so enchanted by what we learn in the secular world that we bring it into our churches. We strategize, plan, organize, market and measure results according to the wisdom that we learn in our jobs. Even worse, we adapt our theology to accommodate the prevailing world view. Is this correct? It may be helpful to re-examine our views in order to differentiate between what is tradition and that which may well be in line with the Bible, or neutral, or diametrically opposed to biblical principles.

Surely, Christian beliefs are not reserved for Sundays but must be applied '24/7'—365. In this respect, we can glorify God in many ways and can be 'salt and light' in our society. Wayne Grudem[4] says:

# Introduction

One way we can glorify God is often overlooked. This additional way to glorify God is the key to understanding why God made the world the way he did. It is also the key to understanding why God gave us the moral commands he did. And it is the key to understanding why human beings have an instinctive drive to work, to be productive, to earn and save and give, and to the thousands of specific activities that fill our days. This additional way to glorify God is *imitation*—imitation of the attributes of God.

Why do we see our jobs as outside of our Christian beliefs? Ryken[5] traces man's attitude to work, showing that in Greco-Roman philosophy work was not regarded as fit for a free man. The root word in Greek for work is the same as the word for sorrow! Then came the Roman Catholic medieval thinking of dualism, i.e. work which was done by the clergy and that done by the laity, with the former being more important. This thinking was changed during the Enlightenment and even Roman Catholic writers such as Thomas Moore began to see what was called 'the dignity of labour'. The Reformation and, subsequently, the Puritans made the greatest impact to change man's thinking by introducing what is referred to as the 'Protestant work ethic' (or the 'Puritan work ethic'). The Reformation saw all work as sacred and done for the glory of God. The Enlightenment produced the secular humanistic view of work which laid the foundation for the modern view that work is a necessary evil to fund people's needs and to satisfy the desire for materialism. Consequently, even when we see the virtues of *the work ethic* being extolled, we should be wary because the purpose of work in the secular world is purely economic. As Christians, we include much more in the work ethic, as we shall see later.

Our discovery of God's intentions for our jobs must start with the Bible. If this conflicts with secular thought, then we must be prepared to be 'countercultural' and accept the consequences.

So, far from taking our secular learning into the church, we must seek to find absolute principles (i.e. those which apply to all situations) in the Bible and apply them to our work situations, unless the Bible limits the instructions to the church. Perhaps, those working in churches, Christian charities or missions may be fortunate and already operating within a biblical world view. It will, nevertheless, be helpful for them to evaluate their work practices to discover if they are indeed being biblical.

Most of us have probably determined that we will pursue biblical principles such as honesty and diligence in our work. That is a good start, but we need to go much further and determine what other practices may require a new approach. This book will also seek to refine our views even about the 'givens' such as integrity and honesty.

The Bible does give some specific instructions for work (and we shall discover them) but we must also apply *all biblical truths* regarding behaviour to the specifics of work. For example, the Bible does not specify a law prohibiting sexual harassment at work but in the seventh commandment it does say, 'You shall not commit adultery' (Exodus 20:14). Jesus went further, forbidding our even thinking about it! (See Matthew 5:27–30.) On the other hand, women are exhorted to 'adorn themselves in respectable apparel, with modesty…' (1 Timothy 2:9). We can, therefore, use these two general principles to develop a Bible-based policy on harassment and dress. Such a policy is not based on political correctness even though it may end up coinciding with some secular views. It is biblical truth applied. We shall look for other such general principles.

A twenty-first century movement among evangelical Christians is to regard the workplace as a major mission field. (There are movements in various countries but I am familiar with 'Getting God to Work' in the UK.[6]) This is encouraged throughout this book. It follows from the general principle that our chief duty is 'to glorify God'. How do we do this? By living in accordance with God's Word in all we do and by pointing men and women to Christ. We shall develop the view that God's *economic plan* for our paid employment is to earn a living and to care for the world. But God's *overall plan* for all of us is to glorify him, notably in evangelism, through our lifestyle and testimony. In writing to Titus, Paul is even more forthright: 'Slaves are to be submissive to their own masters in everything; they are to be well-pleasing, not argumentative, not pilfering, but showing all good faith, so that in everything they may adorn the doctrine of God our Saviour' (Titus 2:9–10). The *NIV* translates the last sentence: '… so that in every way they will make the teaching about God our Saviour attractive.' This is our mission at work.

# Introduction

Here is the acid test: is your manager or a colleague more likely to follow Christ as a result of the way you work? This may sound like a revolutionary view. If it is, then perhaps you regard your job as the major activity in your life and your faith as an 'add on', mainly for Sundays. You may need to change your self-perception, seeing yourself first and foremost as a sinner saved by grace, bought with a price, as one set apart, and then as a worker.

I commence the book with a simple explanation of classical economics and how it should be adapted to meet biblical standards—with apologies to professional economists! Why? It is to establish the centrality of productive work in Christian economics. This makes legitimate our earning an income at work. We also need to define those business activities that are themselves legitimate and, therefore, provide work which can be glorifying to God. The Bible mentions a wide range of activities which constitute work: gardening and farming (the first industry), arts and crafts, soldiering, building and carpentry, tent making, trading, dying fabric, banking, fishing, preaching, the law and even tax collecting. The list is almost endless. There are very few activities that are condemned but there are some that are clearly wrong. How can we know? Any industry which is based on sin (such as prostitution, thieving, gambling) does not provide an avenue for work but for sinning and is, therefore, not an option for a Christian—or anyone else!

Some readers may be surprised at the extent to which I shall endeavour to base all of my thoughts on the teachings of the Bible but, on the other hand, also offer practical advice on salaries, pensions, investments and so forth. This is because I believe that we should always seek to exhaust biblical material before embarking on pragmatic action and, then, only if such action is not contradicted by the Bible. However, we all need to make sound practical decisions following prayer and careful consideration.

# Work and a Christian view of economics

When God created the world, He caused it to function according to what is known as 'natural law'. Things have continued to function in a predictable and uniform way which lead us to expect 'laws' that govern the material world. It is easy to understand this in the physical world where we readily accept the verdict of scientific laws—even when science itself is not one hundred per cent certain! If we doubt the law of gravity and jump off a building, we quickly discover its absolute truth. The Bible does not set out these laws because it is not a scientific text book, but it simply assumes them. Paul accepted that we could learn directly from nature. Please note what he had to say, 'Does not nature itself teach you ...' (1 Corinthians 11:14). Admittedly, this is about a man's hair, but he does invoke the principle.

The same absolute laws govern the economic and all other realms, as we shall see with respect to human behaviour. In general, economists and psychologists have experienced more difficulty than physical scientists in discovering these laws because they are heavily dependent on human behaviour. Human responses are rather less predictable and less uniform than physical behaviour. But we do need to understand human nature to understand both economic laws and the theory of management.

Therefore, just as we accept the basic laws of physics, so we can accept certain 'natural' laws of economics and human behaviour. We shall commence by looking for those laws which are explicitly stated in the Bible, for other laws which are assumed in the Bible and for others which may be refuted. Clearly, the first two categories are the ones which we can accept.

## Basic economic laws

### ADAM SMITH

No summary of economics would be complete without referring to

Adam Smith, generally regarded as the founder of modern liberal economics. We should, however, understand that he was critical of Christians and other religions. Smith was not a capitalist in that he saw people and not money as the most important resource. His motivation was to improve the lot of the common people and was, therefore, entirely utilitarian in his motive. Smith did not have all the answers and sometimes contradicted himself but he did postulate three very important principles in his *Wealth of Nations* published in 1776. He believed that a free society, especially one in which the markets were completely free, would bring prosperity to all. Note his emphasis on material well-being. (We would argue that a society that seeks to live according to the Bible will bring God's blessing, whatever that may be.) Smith saw the role of government as providing security for its citizens, including the security of maintaining a free market. He argued that the state should only do that which free enterprise could not do. In recent years, Smith has become more acceptable. Leading economists have written several books reviving his work.[1]

Smith's principles were:

*A free market*. Smith believed passionately in *an international free market*. Oddly, he did not relate this to the determination of the value of a product (he was less concerned about services than we are), but to such matters as import duties, allocation of resources and freedom of labour.

*Division of labour*. We would use the term 'specialization' or in Christian jargon, 'distribution of gifts'. He used the example of manufacturing a pin, pointing out that if anyone tried to do the whole job himself, he would have to mine the ore, reduce it to iron, work it into a pin—an endless process. We can accept this law as it is a biblical principle, provided that it does not lead to inhuman conditions of work. The Industrial Revolution led to industries which continue into the twenty-first century (now mainly in the developing world) in which specialization created boring, repetitive work undermining human dignity. If the sole purpose of work is to advance economic welfare, without restraint then, child labour, excessive hours or unhealthy working conditions will follow, even slavery. Lord Shaftesbury, William Wilberforce and others demonstrated Christian concern in fighting to rectify such wrongs on men and women created in God's image. We must go on looking for such abuses of otherwise sound economic laws.

*Self-interest.* By this Smith did not mean selfishness, and a recurring lesson in his writings was that we should not be greedy. Smith wrote another book, *The Theory of Moral Sentiments*, published in 1759. In it he said that each one of us 'is first and principally recommended to his own care'. What he meant was that men should accept responsibility for their own income and welfare. On the surface this is none other than what we shall set out later from 2 Thessalonians 3:6–12 and 1 Timothy 5:8, namely, that we are to work to support ourselves and our families. But carried to its logical conclusion and, without any restraints from the Bible, this principle simply leads to self-indulgence and greed.

Although Smith made no attempt to base his laws on the Bible, he did write of man being made in God's image and believed that man was different from the animals. He did not believe man to be innately good. Nor does the Bible teach that. He also endorsed the principle of fair exchange quoted below. He put these two views together rather humorously: 'Nobody ever saw a dog make a fair and deliberate exchange of one bone for another with another dog.'[2]

Smith also taught that work embraces 'skill, dexterity and judgement'. Man's work differs from animals in that it is capable of responding to challenges requiring human judgement, i.e. conscious thought. Human beings possess these skills *because* they are made in God's image. Work done by human beings is also capable of being creative, another result of being made in God's image. Work is, therefore, *meaningful* in addition to being utilitarian.

Smith's principles are close to what I have called 'natural law' because the abovementioned three laws are consistent with what is either endorsed or assumed in the Bible. But he failed to see the biblical constraints which Christian economics require. We shall, therefore, build on this base but will add some biblical constraints as we go along.

**FREEDOM**

The first assumption that I expound in the next few paragraphs is that individuals are free, but are not without boundaries. There are always limits to freedom. This principle is held by secular thinkers but we are interested in the biblical constraints as defined by Jesus, 'So Jesus said to the Jews who had believed in him, "If you abide in my word, you are truly my disciples, and you will know the truth, and the truth will set you free"'(John 8:31–32). Peter had this to say, 'Live as people who are free, not using your freedom as a cover-up for evil, but living as servants of God' (1 Peter 2:16). The point of these statements is that God intended people to live a life of indivisible freedom. However, after Adam sinned, we all lost our freedom and became slaves to sin. Only when we become Christians do we regain our freedom. The nature of this freedom, however, is not the right to arbitrary choice nor a life of lasciviousness. The passages above make it clear that we are free to live the way God intended, abiding in his word. Adam and Eve were free but were forbidden to touch certain trees. It is the same now. The limits to freedom are defined by all of God's laws, including the natural laws of economics set out below.

## THE MARKET

A free market is where we establish a fair price for any article or service. Attempts, such as communism, to find any other method have all failed. This is largely because they hold an unreasonable view of the wishes of the individual. God cares about us as individuals and allows us certain freedoms. The market gives us one such freedom. The market exists where a willing seller exchanges goods or services with a willing buyer. The key issue in the market is that it must be *free,* permitting competition. One of the realities of life is that few people or organizations actually want the market to be free. They would rather it be tipped in their favour, so, as a consequence, they proceed to intervene. Governments love doing so, always under the guise of altruism but, in reality, they do this to increase their power or simply to win the next election. Business, the professions and all those who believe that they can tip the market in their favour also try to intervene. Businesses try to influence the market either by lobbying for a change in the law (such as the pharmaceutical companies in the USA) or by cornering a section of the market and gaining undue market power. Government's real role in all of this is, as always, to protect its citizens. In this case, the protection should be from those who seek to interfere with a truly free market, and that includes government itself. Consequently, the concept of a truly free market becomes a myth.

Free market economists argue that in a free market competition prevents unfair advantage, exploitation or overpricing. However, the real, fallen world does not function that way and hence *restraint* is called for. This introduces another law, the law of *fair exchange*. This is none other than the principle of '… as you wish that others would do to you, do so to them' (Luke 6:31). Fair exchange assumes that the parties are equally strong and, therefore, the outcome is balanced. However, this seldom arises in practice. Often one party has more bargaining power than the other and is, therefore, tempted to use this power to the detriment of the weaker party. To prevent this, Old Testament laws forbad taking advantage of the poor by not even permitting interest to be charged on loans to other Israelites (Exodus 22:25). The Christian approach, therefore, requires that the more powerful party never pushes its advantage to the utmost. A good test of this is for the parties to imagine that if the roles were reversed, both parties would still feel that they had done a good deal (Luke 6:31). The Christian view of the market place is, therefore, one subject to *restraint or limitation*.

While we are not given specific instructions about the market in the Bible, both the Old and New Testaments simply assume its existence. See Ezekiel 27:24, Matthew 20:3 and 1 Corinthians 10:25.

**THE LAW OF SUPPLY AND DEMAND**

The law of supply and demand places a higher value on goods or services which are scarce and a lower price when goods and services become plentiful. We see a dramatic illustration of this in the Bible when Samaria was under siege (2 Kings 6:25; 7:1). Produce reached ridiculous prices in the siege due to shortage but immediately afterwards fell back to what must have been a normal price. This law, in turn, will give rise to *non-uniformity* in the value of goods and services, including *inequality* in earnings. The Bible assumes this. Notice that the disciples determined 'everyone according to his ability, to send relief …' (Acts 11:29). Not all were equally rich and their giving reflected their *unequal* means. This law of inequality in riches is assumed by Paul because he gave one set of instructions to those who *sought* to be rich and a different set to those who *were* rich (1 Timothy 6:9, 17–19).

### BIBLE-BASED ECONOMIC LAWS

The abovementioned are important natural laws which are assumed in the Bible. The Bible also gives us further economic laws which are absolutely explicit. We now look at these laws insofar as they set out the *legitimate sources* of income or wealth.

### PROPERTY

Anyone may own property, fixed, moveable or intellectual (but not other people). This follows directly from the eighth commandment: 'You shall not steal' (Exodus 20:15). There can be no stealing if there is no ownership. Many economic systems (such as communism) have tried to break this principle and achieved about the same result as if one tried to break the law of gravity.

### THE GIFT OF WEALTH

God created the world with inbuilt wealth and hence the capacity to generate income. Wealth is found in creation: 'A river flowed out of Eden to water the garden … where there is gold' (Genesis 2:10–11). Moreover, as part of his universal grace, God intends us to share in this wealth.

Consider these passages:

'Everyone also to whom God has given wealth and possessions and power to enjoy them, and to accept his lot and rejoice in his toil—this is the gift of God' (Ecclesiastes 5:19).

Solomon goes on in the book of Proverbs to say, 'The hand of the diligent makes rich' (Proverbs 10:4).

Taken together, these verses show that the gift of wealth is properly accumulated though diligent work. Moving on to the New Testament, notice what Jesus had to say about the practical things which our Father knows we need. He said, 'But seek first the kingdom of God and his righteousness, and all *these things* will be added to you' (Matthew 6:33, emphasis mine).

As we have already seen, Paul assumed that some Christians would be wealthy and, therefore, gave specific instructions about how they were to handle their riches (1 Timothy 6:17–19). He did not tell them to give up their riches. We see this more clearly in the Old Testament in the covenant with Abram where God included material blessings: 'And I will make of you a great nation, and I will bless you …' (Genesis 12:2). The blessing here clearly included material blessings as we see in the following chapter in Genesis: 'Now Abram was very rich in livestock, in silver, and in gold' (Genesis 13:2). It is important to note that this interpretation is confirmed in Deuteronomy where we have a commentary on the covenant: 'You shall remember the Lord your God, for it is he who gives you power to get wealth, *that he may confirm his covenant that he swore to your fathers*' (Deuteronomy 8:17–18, emphasis mine). I am not suggesting that the covenant as stated above can be directly applied to Christians today, but it does tell us about the *nature* of God and his view of wealth. We can, therefore, conclude that there is nothing wrong with wealth; it is one of God's great gifts to mankind. Its *misuse* is the problem, as we shall see later.

There is, however, a fine line between legitimately acquired wealth, properly used, and greed. We will have to grapple with this distinction because greed is a sin, riches are not. Read what Jesus said: 'Woe to you, scribes and Pharisees, hypocrites! For you clean the outside of the cup and the plate, but inside they are full of *greed and self-indulgence*' (Matthew 23:25, emphasis mine). And read the words of the apostle Paul too: 'But now I am writing to you not to associate with anyone who bears the name of brother if he is guilty of sexual immorality or *greed*, or is an *idolater*, reviler, drunkard, or swindler—not even to eat with such a one' (1 Corinthians 5:11, emphasis mine). Moreover, many companies employ greed as the means of motivating employees. You, my reader, may be in this position or you may be required to manage a team whose motivation is based on greed.

**THE WORK ETHIC**

The command to work follows directly from being made in God's image. God is a working God and we glorify him when we copy what he did, namely, to work six days and then rest for one (Exodus 20:9). The day of rest is as important as the command to work. (For a full treatment of both work and leisure see *Work and Leisure in Christian Perspective* by Lelend Ryken[3].) God left no room for doubt on this subject. The fourth commandment has two positive statements: keep the Sabbath Day holy and work for six days. The commandment went on to explain God's reason. It was the way in which God worked in creation. (See Exodus 20:9.) What does the New Testament have to say? Jesus lived about thirty-three years on this earth. Only three years were spent in 'full-time ministry', probably eighteen were as a builder/carpenter. He would have started at the lowest level as some sort of apprentice. It seems probable that his earthly father, Joseph, died during this time and, as the eldest son, he would have had to assume his father's responsibilities. So, was Jesus a manager as well? Note that Jesus was not only the Son of God, but also the second person of the Trinity—that is, God himself. 'But Jesus answered them, "My Father is working until now, and I am working"'(John 5:17). As image bearers of God, we are to imitate Him and work as God and Jesus did.

We see that this command to work was given even before Adam sinned: 'The LORD God took the man and put him in the garden of Eden to work it and keep it' (Genesis 2:15). Notice the double command: to *work* and to *keep* the earth. The latter command literally means 'to exercise great care' and is the basis of our responsibility to care for the world. However, a discussion of this subject is not within the scope of this book. The former command literally means 'to serve'. The work was to serve the garden—that is, make sure that the garden prospered. This work was to be a *pleasure* because sin had not yet entered the world and, therefore, nothing would have troubled Adam.

As this book is intended for every working person, we must ask if the command to work applies equally to men and to women? The Bible uses the term 'man' or 'mankind' to mean both men and women as in 'Male and female he created them, and he blessed them and named them Man when *they* were created' (Genesis 5:2, emphasis mine). I shall, therefore, do the same and when I use the term 'man' or 'mankind' or the modern equivalent 'human beings', I mean both men and women because the Bible does so except when a gender specific term is used or the context indicates the gender. The Bible also makes it quite clear that both men and women are made in God's image (Genesis 1:27). We work because this is one of the ways in which both men and women bear that image. In Genesis 2:15 the term used is 'Adam', meaning 'mankind'. It is the same word as the one used in Genesis 5:1–2 (see above) where it explains that the word means both man and woman. This name was given to Adam before the Fall and before Eve was created—that is, to Adam as the *representative* of the human race. We read next of Eve being made out of Adam with a very clear explanation that she was the same 'flesh'. 'Then the man said, "This at last is bone of my bones and flesh of my flesh; she shall be called Woman, because she was taken out of Man"'(Genesis 2:23–24). We also read that Eve was to be a 'helper': 'Then the LORD God said, "It is not good that the man should be alone; I will make him a helper fit for him"'(Genesis 2:18). She was to work with Adam.

It is, therefore, not unreasonable to assume that the instruction was given to men and women. However, to be certain of this, we need to see this happening repeatedly as we progress through the Old and New Testaments. The first clue we are given is after the Fall: 'To the woman he said, "I will surely multiply your pain in childbearing; in pain you shall bring forth children. Your desire shall be for your husband, and he shall rule over you"'(Genesis 3:16). The woman's primary work would be as a wife and mother—call it a homemaker—and indeed this is what we see throughout the Bible. Note Paul's teaching in the New Testament: 'Older women likewise are to … teach what is good, and so train the young women to love their husbands and children, to be self-controlled, pure, *working at home*, kind, and submissive to their own husbands, that the word of God may not be reviled' (Titus 2:3–5, emphasis mine).

But if we need further confirmation, consider Proverbs chapter 31. This is an interesting portion of the book of Proverbs because it is set out as absolute truth compared to many of the parts of the book which often express relative truths—that is, 'rather this… than that…' Note the teaching of the passage: 'She rises while it is yet night and provides food for her household and portions for her maidens' (v. 15) and 'She looks well to the ways of her household and does not eat the bread of idleness. Her children rise up and call her blessed; her husband also, and he praises her' (Proverbs 31:27–28).

No one can doubt that this woman is a good homemaker. But it does not stop there. No, consider what else she does. 'She seeks wool and flax, and works with willing hands... She considers a field and buys it; with the fruit of her hands she plants a vineyard... She perceives that her merchandise is profitable. Her lamp does not go out at night. She puts her hands to the distaff, and her hands hold the spindle. She opens her hand to the poor and reaches out her hands to the needy' (Proverbs 31:13–20). She is a merchant; she manufactures; she trades; she farms; and she practises what we call charity. In short, she works in all the ways that a man may work.

Following accepted principles of interpretation, we now turn to other passages in the New Testament to find more examples of such women. Consider Priscilla, wife of Aquila. They were both tentmakers, obviously working together (Acts 18:1–3). Another example is Lydia who was a 'seller of purple goods' (Acts 16:14). So women also worked and, while their primary role may have been that of homemakers, they did do other work as well. In my own family, I have two daughters and two daughters-in-law. All are professionals and all run homes that seek to glorify God. All, at some time, have fitted in a certain amount of professional work into their family schedules. I have no doubt some of them will return to professional work when their children are grown up. This fits the biblical pattern.

This law, known as the 'Protestant work ethic', is central to all Bible-based economics, all wealth creation and all poverty eradication. In the Bible, we are given further teaching that it is by work that God *distributes* his wealth to us. Let us consider these passages: 'You shall remember the LORD your God, for it is he who gives you power to get wealth' (Deuteronomy 8:18). 'A slack hand causes poverty, but the hand of the diligent makes rich' (Proverbs 10:4). Note that 'a slack hand' (one that does not work) results in poverty. Also note Proverbs 13:4: 'The soul of the sluggard craves and gets nothing, while the soul of the diligent is richly supplied'; and Proverbs 13:11 as it is written in the *King James Version*: 'Wealth gotten by vanity shall be diminished: but he that gathereth by labour shall increase'; '... for the labourer deserves his wages' (Luke 10:7); '... and to work with your hands, as we instructed you, so that you may live properly before outsiders and be dependent on no one' (1 Thessalonians 4:11–12).

From these passages, we can conclude that God's second purpose for work is to earn a living. Work in a community of other workers is called a 'company' which leads to the concept of a business as we know it. Wayne Grudem[4] in his book *Business for the Glory of God* shows that a business operating properly glorifies God. We must not consider business and, therefore, 'secular' employment as a 'necessary evil', but rather as the outworking of God's *economic plan* for mankind. In this respect, it is no different from so-called 'full-time service'. All work is full-time service for God.

**WORK BECOMES TOIL**

Work, however, changed its nature after Adam sinned. Adam was expelled from the Garden of Eden where everything was perfect and was told that henceforth work would become 'toil'. Adam would do battle with weeds even as today we do battle with all the adversities that we encounter in our workplace. This struggle also introduced poverty for, thereafter, man's efforts would sometimes produce imperfect results. Read what God said to Adam after he and Eve had sinned: '... cursed is the ground because of you; *in pain you shall eat of it all the days of your life; thorns and thistles it shall bring forth* for you; and you shall eat the plants of the field. By *the sweat of your face* you shall eat bread...' (Genesis 3:17–19, emphasis mine).

Man lost his freedom and became a slave to created things. As a result, he suffers along with all creation. 'For the creation was subjected to futility' (Romans 8:20). 'For we know that the whole creation has been groaning together in the pains of childbirth until now. And not only the creation, but we ourselves, who have the firstfruits of the Spirit, groan inwardly ...' (Romans 8:22–23). We suffer along with all creation. Not all work will be satisfying and enjoyable even though it is still ordained of God.

Before the Fall, work was a pleasure, an expression of our status as God's image bearers. After the Fall, it became necessary to earn a living. Notwithstanding this change, work still brings fulfilment and can be satisfying: 'Behold, what I have seen to be good and fitting is to eat and drink *and find enjoyment in all the toil with which one toils* under the sun the few days of his life that God has given him, for this is his lot' (Ecclesiastes 5:18, emphasis mine). The expression 'toiling under the sun' is used throughout the book of Ecclesiastes to mean 'on the earth'. It describes our situation.

We have no other choice but to work. This is also spelled out in the New Testament. 'Let the thief no longer steal, but rather let him labour, doing honest work with his own hands ...' (Ephesians 4:28). Even stronger was Paul's warning in 2 Thessalonians 3:10. Taken together with Paul's concern for those in need (2 Corinthians chapters 8, 9 and following), it is not that Paul is really advocating people starving to death, rather he is establishing the seriousness of the link between work and sustaining ourselves.

The term 'work ethic' is frequently used in a secular context largely because work is a necessary condition for an economy to flourish. We would expect this to be true since it is a creation ordinance and, therefore, just as breathing is necessary for life, so work is necessary for economic life. But the secular concept of work is purely utilitarian—that is, it exists to earn a living or for feeding greed. We shall expand on these differences later.

### OTHER LEGITIMATE SOURCES OF WEALTH

Not all of the sources of wealth recorded for us in the Bible are relevant to our topic but for completeness and in order to establish *non-legitimate* sources of wealth, I shall list them briefly:

### PROFIT

Some Christian writers scorn the so-called 'profit motive'. But is it wrong? The Bible does not say so except for the purpose of forbidding the exploitation of poor fellow Israelites through charging interest. Some references endorse profit. Note the case of the virtuous woman of Proverbs 31: 'She perceives that her merchandise is profitable' (Proverbs 31:18). We are told that 'in all toil there is profit' (Proverbs 14:23). James cites an example of a person going to a city to do business: 'Come now, you who say, "Today or tomorrow we will go into such and such a town and spend a year there and trade and make a profit"' (James 4:13). He does not condemn the trading nor the making of a profit, but he condemns the act of ignoring God's sovereignty. Admittedly, this is argued from silence, but can we imagine James using such an example if it were wrong? The issue for Christians is *restraint* as opposed to *greed*. Profit in a business is needed to fund the growth of the business and to generate a legitimate return on the investment. However, profits must be generated by observing the principle of fair exchange and all of the behavioural principles outlined in subsequent chapters.

Some businesses are set up as 'mutual societies' in which there are no shareholders and the organization is classified as 'not for profit'. All benefits pass to the clients. On the surface, this sounds good (and sometimes *is* good). Typical examples are building societies (mortgage lenders or 'thrifts'), banks, insurance and health insurance businesses. Some (certainly not all) are often characterized by inefficiency and low standards. Over the past few decades, many 'mutual societies' have converted to normal profit-making companies with shareholders. The results are often a marked increase in efficiency and improved customer service. I recently researched health insurance in the UK and discovered that the rates of the 'for profit' companies were in general considerably lower than those of the mutual societies. However, as we have noted elsewhere, we live in a real, sinful world in which greed is one of the most common sins encountered in business. Restraint is necessary. The government must play a role and, as always, this is to protect its citizens. This calls for laws, regulations and policing of all businesses. A good example of a government doing its job was the fining of the insurance company UNUM.[5] (This was the largest fine in insurance company history imposed in California.) Claims were unjustifiably declined in pursuit of profits. Competition will eventually force companies to honour their policies, but this takes too long and hence the need for regulation and, if necessary, prosecution. The 'dark side' of capitalism is the making of profit by whatever means possible. Christians should, therefore, be wary of endorsing unqualified capitalism.

In the final analysis, reasonable profit may be a sensible measure of a business' success and produce a legitimate return on investment, but it must always be secondary to the primary purpose of glorifying God through service.

### RETURN ON INVESTMENT

In the parable of the distribution of the talents, Jesus indirectly endorsed a *return on investment*, either through running some sort of business or, at the very least, through interest from a bank (Matthew 25:27). No one will invest in a business that shows no return. As Jesus taught, rather put the money in a bank where interest would be earned. It is also important to note that most companies use a large portion of their profits for re-investment which allows the company to grow, thereby creating, inter alia, more jobs. Without profit this becomes impossible.

### INHERITANCE

The Bible also endorses inheritance as a legitimate source of income. Early in the establishment of the nation of Israel, God introduced inheritance for all the tribes, except the Levites (Numbers 26:53). Throughout the Old Testament, the concept of inheritance is repeated again and again as we see from Proverbs 13:22: 'A good man leaves an inheritance to his children's children.' The New Testament endorses the fact of the inheritance given to the Israelites (e.g. Acts 7:5; 13:19) and simply assumes the practice in narratives such as the prodigal son (Luke 15:11–32).

### GIFTS

Finally, gifts or presents are an allowable form of income in the hands of worthy recipients. The most obvious are the gifts given to the poor and needy to help them out of their distress. Paul deals with this extensively in 2 Corinthians 8 and 9. Note what he says, '*Your* abundance at the present time should supply their need, so that *their* abundance may supply *your* need, that there may be fairness' (2 Corinthians 8:14, emphasis mine). Clearly, he was not thinking of long-term dependency because he visualized the time when the tables would be turned.

Gifts given out of love, honour or respect also occur in the Bible. A magnificent example is the bringing of gifts by the wise men to the baby Jesus: 'And going into the house they saw the child with Mary his mother, and they fell down and worshipped him. Then, opening their treasures, they offered him gifts, gold and frankincense and myrrh' (Matthew 2:11). These gifts were 'treasures' and clearly valuable. Mary showed her love for the Saviour by pouring out a gift of very expensive perfume on Jesus' feet and was commended for doing so (John 12:3).

Throughout the Old Testament, we read of 'gifts' being given as part of a celebration. One of the most dramatic was the custom started in the time of Esther: '… the month that had been turned for them from sorrow into gladness and from mourning into a holiday; that they should make them days of feasting and gladness, days for sending gifts of food to one another and gifts to the poor' (Esther 9:22).

We now turn to the *non-legitimate* sources of wealth and income:

### NON-LEGITIMATE SOURCES OF WEALTH

If certain sources of income or wealth are legitimate, then logically the opposites must be avoided. Admittedly, this is an argument from silence, but the case for work as the basis of a biblical economy is so strong that surely no one earnestly seeking to follow God's commandments will seek income from non-legitimate sources.

The clearest non-legitimate source of income is theft. This is not based on silence but from the Ten Commandments (Exodus 20:15) and is reinforced in the New Testament: 'Let the thief no longer steal, but rather let him *labour*, doing honest *work* with his own hands' (Ephesians 4:28, emphasis mine). The scope of this book does not permit me to go into details on the subtle ways in which we are tempted to steal, but the reader can explore these further in any number of good books on the Ten Commandments.[6]

Other sources of income which are not biblical are:

### BEGGING AND HANDOUTS

Handouts often begin with some form of begging, even if this is the completing of an application form for financial assistance. Begging does occur in the Bible, but is never condoned. This is different from some religions where begging is seen as a noble occupation. This is not to say that poverty will not occur and, when it does, it is the responsibility of Christians to alleviate it. Both Jesus and Paul taught that we *are* to give handouts when we encounter someone in real and immediate need (Matthew 25:37–40; Romans 12:20). We *must* be caring and concerned about the poor when they cannot help themselves. This has been a distinguishing mark of Christians down the ages. In the first few centuries, it was *the* distinguishing mark of Christians. As a further example, any study of British history of the nineteenth century will show that Christians were often at the forefront of charitable works during the age when the Industrial Revolution and the Empire greatly increased wealth. However, charitable giving must be done sensitively so as not to encourage the recipient to stay out of work, nor must the handout infringe the recipient's dignity as one made in the image of God (Genesis 1:27). Long-term dependency is demeaning and, therefore, wrong on this count alone.

While the Christian must be concerned about the poor, the poor themselves must not be idle nor wait for others to bail them out. It is worth considering the passage found in 2 Thessalonians 3:6–12:

Now we command you, brothers, in the name of our Lord Jesus Christ, that you keep away from any brother who is walking in idleness and not in accord with the tradition that you received from us. For you yourselves know how you ought to imitate us, because we were not idle when we were with you, nor did we eat anyone's bread without paying for it, but with toil and labour we worked night and day, that we might not be a burden to any of you. It was not because we do not have that right, but to give you in ourselves an example to imitate. For even when we were with you, we would give you this command: If anyone is not willing to work, let him not eat. For we hear that some among you walk in idleness, not busy at work, but busybodies. Now such persons we command and encourage in the Lord Jesus Christ to do their work quietly and to earn their own living.

Paul was writing at a time when 'benefactors' supported 'clients' who in turn became supporters of the benefactor. These clients did no real work but would say whatever favoured the benefactor. Paul called them 'busybodies'. Note that Paul was entitled to be paid for preaching the gospel but, in contrast to the busybodies, he set an example by performing his trade and supporting himself. He gave a frank warning that if they did not start working then they should not be given food. Paul was not being harsh nor was he advocating starvation (that would be in contradiction to many other exhortations he gave) but he wanted to emphasize the importance of work. The benefactors of the first century have roughly been replaced by the welfare state, and I am convinced that Paul would give the same warning to those who live on state grants.

The unemployed must seek productive work. There is no other lasting solution to poverty. John F. Kennedy was correct when he introduced the slogan: 'Give a hand, not a handout.' Regrettably, modern governments do not heed this advice and continue to give incentives to people so that they do not work. All statistics show that this route simply fails. This matter can be studied further by reading the works of the noted secular economist, Deepak Lal.[7]

George Grant in his book *Bringing in the Sheaves*[8] quotes some alarming statistics for the USA. He shows that following the start of the war on poverty by President Lyndon Johnson, poverty actually increased despite huge sums being channelled to its relief. This is because the entire programme is based on handouts which condemns millions to perpetual poverty and *keeps them out of work*. Owing to the generous value of the handouts from one or more of the seventeen programmes then available in the USA, the average equivalent income for many on welfare was found to be about *fifty per cent higher than the minimum wage* paid by such employers as MacDonalds. Who is likely to seek a job if the state's handouts pay more?

In the UK the problem may even be greater. I was recently told by a businessman with whom I had lunch that his daughter was the single parent of two children. She was drawing from all the programmes to which she was *entitled* and he had calculated that for her to work and earn the same amount, she would need a job which paid more than *double* the minimum wage.

No support must be given to anyone if this reduces the individual's *sense of responsibility* for his own welfare and that of his family. Read what Paul had to say: 'But if anyone does not provide for his relatives, and especially for members of his household, he has denied the faith and is worse than an unbeliever' (1 Timothy 5:8). One of the evils of our day is the belief that we can behave as we choose, 'eating and drinking and making merry', and then cast ourselves upon the state to look after us in our later years or in times of unemployment. There is no morality in behaving like this. Nor may we assume that it is morally acceptable for the state to play Robin Hood by robbing the rich to fund the people made poor because they have been encouraged to stay out of work (Ephesians 4:28). It is simply organized theft for the state to rob the rich to fund the idle.

This book does not aim to deal with welfare and relief of poverty. I recommend that readers obtain a copy of George Grant's book *Bringing in the Sheaves* because of its biblical basis and its practical outworking in a real and successful church-based solution.

### GAMBLING, COMPETITIONS AND OTHER 'GET-RICH' SCHEMES

Gambling is also wrong as a substitute for work. This includes all forms of gambling, including *betting, raffles, bingo* and *competitions* which are not based on meaningful work. Many competitions introduce some element of *apparent* work with the intention of legitimizing the competition. Even if we are fooled by this sort of sleight of hand, God is certainly not misled. The basis of all these schemes is *greed without work*, which we have already condemned as sin.

Many 'get-rich' schemes, such as the pyramid investments, are dressed up to look like an investment but are also simply greed without work. Deposits which are based on a return on investment either in a bank or in shares or property are not gambling but investments, albeit with various degrees of risk. How is it possible to tell the difference? Gambling does not give everyone the *same* return but all of the winnings go to a few 'lucky' winners purely on the basis of chance, while all of the others simply lose. A genuine investment may be at a high level of risk, provided that it is accompanied by a higher rate of return. But it is not a gamble if everyone who makes the same investment stands to earn the same income (or loss) and if it is based on a calculated risk which examines all of the facts. It is also a matter of the person's intent. If the motive is covetousness and greed rather than a desire to be a good steward, then the activity needs to be reconsidered.

### RIGHT WING OR LEFT WING?

Are Christians communists, as some have argued, or capitalists, as many others have tried to affirm? I would argue that we are neither, nor are we part of the new 'Progressive Movement', even if we find ourselves in sympathy with many of its views. This is largely because our motives are always different from secular economic objectives. Some Christian principles such as the free market coincide with capitalism (within the scope of the boundaries discussed earlier) but others such as concern for the poor may be more in line with the progressive movement or even a superficial understanding of socialism. Nor can we endorse a totally free market bereft of any limits or restraints such as that proposed by Deepak Lal in his otherwise excellent book *Reviving the Invisible Hand*.[8] We are Christians and should not be pigeonholed into any man-made stereotype. At all times, we are motivated by love for Christ and his glory, and constrained by the principles of Christian behaviour.

Unrestrained socialism is also not biblical. It tends to institutionalize care and concern. It also emphasizes *rights* rather than *responsibilities*. Rights can only be earned as one half of an agreement with an employer, but the other half will be *responsibility*—that is, the work that we do in return for the *rights* that we enjoy as employees. We have no automatic, one-sided rights simply because we exist. Indeed, before God we have no rights at all. All we deserve as sinners is death. (See Romans 6:23.) It is only because of God's grace and on the basis of Jesus' work on the cross that 'rights' are recovered. And these rights have to do with our rights as citizens of a heavenly kingdom.

Socialism also teaches *entitlements*, often without the need for any work at all. Welfare has become so accepted in secular thinking that few question the serious departure from biblical principles that our society which is driven by entitlements assumes. Governments simply pay welfare if a person does not have a job. Generally, there is only a weak requirement even to seek employment. Welfare becomes a substitute for work. This is in direct conflict with the biblical work ethic described above. As we have already argued, Christians must be concerned for the poor, the unemployed and the destitute but our focus should be *to get them into work*. There are many jobs which are left undone in our societies because authorities do not have the money to pay for people to do them. They do not have the money precisely because they have diverted public funds to keeping the very same people *out of work* through welfare! People who are out of work and on welfare should be required to perform some community service such as cleaning hospitals, schools or public spaces while they are on welfare. Then it ceases to be welfare. The Bible stresses *responsibility* and *work*, warning that if anyone does not work that person should also not eat (2 Thessalonians 3:10).

Much of what we have looked at coincides to a degree with various secular views and may even be politically correct, but this is not what drives us. 'Political correctness' is a shifting sand which changes with every generation. God does not change and nor does his teaching.

Perhaps, if we do accept any label for our view of economics, it is that we believe in *free enterprise within the boundaries set by biblical principles*.

## Summary of chapter 1

Christian economics is based on a Christian culture or world view which emphasizes that riches are not wrong nor poverty virtuous. 'The Lord makes poor and makes rich ...' (1 Samuel 2:7). All that we have comes from God. Greed is roundly condemned and, instead, we are to learn contentment regardless of our situation. Read what the Apostle Paul has to say: 'I have learned in whatever situation I am to be content' (Philippians 4:11).

The basic law of economics found in the Bible is that we must work because in this way we demonstrate that we are made in God's image. Mankind was created to work diligently and thereby to earn a living and to care for the world. This was ordained by God before man fell into sin. Work only changed its nature from being a pleasure to 'toil' after Adam had sinned.

There are several legitimate sources of income and all others are to be rejected.

Work is a major opportunity to glorify God and to proclaim the gospel. It must not become an avenue to satisfy our greed.

### Case study

Software companies invest large sums of 'venture capital' in developing software. Some companies have developed software which has become a household product with many millions of copies sold. Assume that to develop such a product will cost £10 million and that the product is launched at £100 per copy. The cost of reproducing a copy is a mere £1 and the company overheads amount to £20 million per annum. The company has no other product to sell.

#### QUESTIONS

1. How many copies must be sold in the first year to recover all the costs?
2. Once the company has recovered all of its costs, is the company justified in selling more copies at the same price of £100? Under what circumstances should it alter its price up or down?
3. What ethical issues should concern a Christian owner of such a business?

DISCUSSION

The total fixed costs that have to be recovered are £10 million plus £20 million = £30 million. Assuming that the costs are recovered in one year at a margin of £99, this means that a total of 303,030 copies must be sold in that first year (30 million/99 = 303,030). After year one, the margin remains at £99 and, as just the fixed costs have to be recovered, only 202,020 copies need be sold each year thereafter. In excess of that quantity, the company is operating at above what is known as the 'breakeven point', and the full margin of £99 per copy will be profit.

Investing £30 million in a new product is extremely risky and the providers of this finance are entitled to a high return because of the higher risk. Jesus endorsed this when he commended the man with the five talents for producing another five and advised the man with the one talent that he might as well have put the talent into the bank where it would have been safe and earned interest. According to the account in the Gospel of Matthew, the return of 5 on an investment of 5 is 100 per cent profit. Jesus never rebuked him for making too much profit; instead he commended him for good stewardship. (In a similar parable in the Gospel of Luke, the gain was 1000 per cent and 500 per cent).

Assume that the product turns out to be very popular and it sells one million copies a year from the second year onwards. This will produce a profit of £79 million each year, representing a massive return on the original £30 million. Is this 'exploiting' the market and the customers?

First of all, we need to apply the principle of 'fair exchange'. Are the buyers happy with paying the £100 price? Do they consider this to be an excessive price or do they consider it to be fair because it is highly valued by them? Can anyone else do it at a lower cost? If they can and the markets are 'free', anyone may compete. Under these circumstances the price must be fair. Selling one million copies a year means that the 'demand' is high and, therefore, the supply will be set at a level which the supplier and the market together considers fair. Otherwise, people will stop buying it until an alternative comes along. The key issue is that the market must be free. The supplier is not obliged to drop his price just because he is making a huge profit. He is entitled to a high return because he made a high-risk investment. He will drop his price when he judges that he may be inviting competition.

Some readers will remember that when home computers first came out they used a variety of products such as Visicalc, Word Perfect and Lotus 123. Where are they now? They have been overtaken by other products which the market has produced and which in some way or another offer customers a better price-value relationship.

## Discussion Questions

A. A single mother of two young children cannot find a paying job. She receives welfare which enables her to stay at home and look after her children without being a burden to anyone.
  1. Should she be looking for a job?
  2. Who should be supporting her?
  3. Does her caring for her children constitute *work*?
  4. What biblical principles create a dilemma for her?
  5. Is it wrong for her to be accepting welfare?
B. Is it wrong for anyone to live on welfare? If they have little option, what should they do in order to comply with God's command to work?
C. What should be the role of the church in poverty alleviation?
D. What should the state do?
E. Do careers as professional entertainers and sportsmen and women constitute legitimate work?

# Behaviour at work

I commenced my working life at the lowest level. I did a crammed apprenticeship covering six trades in the steel industry. It was rough and dirty. I can recall working under a steel rolling mill and coming out covered in black grease! At that time, I had not thought through my position on being a Christian at work but a few things became apparent to me even then. One is well summarized as follows: 'Whatever your hand finds to do, do it with your might...' (Ecclesiastes 9:10). I fully intended to learn all I could because I was certain that it was right and, in addition, it would benefit me in later life. I noticed that some of my colleagues took every chance to avoid the hard or dirty jobs and disappeared at every opportune moment. I pitied them because their attitude to work was clearly inadequate. Within ten years, I held a senior management position in that same steelworks. But, as I rose through the ranks, I never saw any of those apprenticeship colleagues again. I suspect that they stayed at the bottom! Was my approach correct and, if it was, was it adequate? We shall examine that in more detail now.

## The nature of mankind

We need to understand the nature of mankind as it is described in the Bible:

### MADE IN GOD'S IMAGE

We have already seen that man (both genders) is made in the image of God. This is one of the pillars on which we build a doctrine of all interpersonal relationships.

What is the significance of this image bearer status of mankind? God explains a little later in Genesis that we must treat one another as special creatures because we are made in his image. Attacking a person is to attack God's image bearer. This is a serious crime. So he says:

From his fellow man I will require a reckoning for the life of man. Whoever sheds the blood of man, by man shall his blood be shed, for God made man in his own image (Genesis 9:5b-6).

Jesus extended this crime to insulting a person: 'You have heard that it was said to those of old, "You shall not murder; and whoever murders will be liable to judgement." But I say to you that everyone who is angry with his brother will be liable to judgement; whoever insults his brother will be liable to the council; and whoever says, "You fool!" will be liable to the hell of fire' (Matthew 5:21–22).

So, we see that because man is made in God's image, we have to respect one another and treat all people, regardless of their status in life, with dignity. It goes even further. Human beings, as the image bearers of God, possess traces of the so-called 'communicable attributes' of God. These are those qualities of God which we can understand because we enjoy to a degree the same attributes. They are: creativity, initiative, individuality, personality, morality, knowledge, intellect, wisdom, power, authority and capacity to work.

Another aspect of being made in his image is that we are made *individuals*. God cares about each one of us *as an individual*. God is one and we are individual too. Hence each person is worthy of individual treatment. Despite the waning of communism, a certain amount of collectivism still prevails in our society. In some circumstances, individuals are expected to give up their individual rights in favour of the majority. This is one of the foundation principles of socialism and is linked to a philosophy known as 'relativism' described in Chapter 3. This makes the individual unimportant relative to the masses. As Christians, we respect *each person* as an individual made in God's image, regardless of how low that person may have sunk or how wicked he may be.

**MANKIND AS SINNERS**

However, being made in God's image is not the complete picture because man has a *dual nature*. Adam was given a free will but succumbed to temptation from the devil. That constitutes the other side of his being. Together with Eve, the first human beings chose to disregard God's commandments and to obey the devil, bringing sin to themselves and all mankind thereafter. Adam and his wife were cursed and driven from the idyllic Garden of Eden to live a life which was to be a struggle. After they had sinned, God said to Adam, 'Cursed is the ground because of you; in pain you shall eat of it all the days of your life; thorns and thistles it shall bring forth for you; and you shall eat the plants of the field. By the sweat of your face you shall eat bread, till you return to the ground, for out of it you were taken' (Genesis 3:17b-19).

The New Testament continues this theme by showing that all people are sinners and sets out some of the consequences of this falling into sin. Paul asks:

'What then? Are we Jews any better off? No, not at all. For we have already charged that all, both Jews and Greeks, are under sin, as it is written: "None is righteous, no, not one; no one understands; no one seeks for God. All have turned aside; together they have become worthless; no one does good, not even one"' (Romans 3:9–12).

He goes on to describe the unregenerate man as:

And you were dead in the trespasses and sins in which you once walked, following the course of this world, following the prince of the power of the air, the spirit that is now at work in the sons of disobedience—among whom we all once lived in the passions of our flesh, carrying out the desires of the body and the mind, and were by nature children of wrath, like the rest of mankind (Ephesians 2:1–3).

This is a pretty damning description of mankind!

### WORKING IN THE REAL WORLD

What has all this to do with the workplace? Everything. It describes the natural behaviour of mankind. It tells us what type of environment to expect in our workplace. It also tells us about our *own default behaviour*—that is, the natural way *we* will react to situations, unless we *consciously* do something different.

We turn now to examine every aspect of this description and list what kind of world we live in:

Firstly, we live in an imperfect, real, sinful world. We should not expect too much. It is fundamental that we remember this basic truth as we proceed to develop an understanding of our work situation.

Secondly, our relationships are damaged. We all break the second great law, namely, to love our neighbour as ourselves (Mark 12:31). My experience is that work colleagues often scheme against—and manipulate—one another to gain some advantage over those that they consider to be competitors. Regrettably, this is often true of Christians and non-Christians alike. It ought not to be so. If we do the best we know how and leave God to give whatever blessing he determines, we shall find much more happiness in our workplace. We should 'strive for peace with everyone' (Hebrews 12:14).

Thirdly, people are self-seeking, ambitious, and often tread ruthlessly upon others to get ahead. Pursuit of career, status and money become the 'norm'. By nature, we want our own way and do not naturally submit to anyone. A powerful characteristic of our age is to ignore authority and reject any prescription as being 'legalism'.

Fourthly, people lust for power. They wish to control others and every situation to their advantage.

Fifthly, greed is often used as the basis of motivation.

Sixthly, by acting in his own selfish interest, mankind breaks every one of God's laws.

The consequences of all this is that mankind cannot be trusted and will need to be controlled and kept from being continually evil in all his actions. Fortunately, God demonstrates grace known as 'common grace' or more correctly 'universal grace' to all mankind. This grace stops us from being absolutely evil all the time and gives us knowledge to control ourselves and our fellow workmates. We shall deal with these matters more fully in later chapters.

## Biblical instructions for the workplace

Notwithstanding the dual nature of man and our natural tendency to sin, we are given specific instructions concerning behaviour in all aspects of life and these must also be applied to our work situation. These instructions are intended for everyone in any position, high or low. If you are a manager, there are special exhortations for you in the next chapter. You need to remember that you, too, are an employee and have someone more senior to whom you are accountable. Consequently, everything that applies to the most junior employee applies to the chairman as well.

Most of what I shall be saying may appear to assume that my readers are in employment, working for someone else. But what of the many who are self-employed? All of these principles still apply (except that they may do as they please with their own money or time, donating it to churches, charities, etc.). They are still to work 'as unto the Lord'. Their service will be to customers, to employees, to providers of service or finance and to their families. They should be motivated by the same (*agape*) love.

Jesus called upon us to be salt and light in the world: 'You are the salt of the earth' (Matthew 5: 13). 'You are the light of the world' (v. 14). 'In the same way, let your light shine before others, so that they may see your good works and give glory to your Father who is in heaven' (v. 16). What does this mean? Salt is that which enhances food. Light is that which enables us to see and, figuratively speaking, to see truth. The Christian must improve the tone of the business by highlighting the truth, righteousness (or justice), fairness and honesty.

Peter says, 'I urge you as sojourners and exiles to abstain from the passions of the flesh… Keep your conduct among the Gentiles honourable, so that when they speak against you as evildoers, *they may see* your good deeds and *glorify God* on the day of visitation' (1 Peter 2:11–12, emphasis mine). Please note the encouragement to evangelize through our *conduct*. Paul calls upon us to do everything to the glory of God. 'So, whether you eat or drink, or whatever you do, do all to the glory of God' (1 Corinthians 10:31). We are to glorify him which means that people will notice God's character in us. This, too, is an evangelistic message.

Before we continue, I shall formulate an important difference between Christian and secular behaviour.

The secular business world is focused on 'outcomes' or results. This is driven by the setting of goals as *required outcomes* for profits, revenue or units to be sold, etc. Various 'inputs' (materials, money, labour, energy, etc.) are then applied to the enterprise and the 'outcomes' are measured and compared to the set goals. To the extent that a deviation occurs in the outcomes, the enterprise steps up its inputs to make sure that the goals are achieved. Viewed from a purely business or economic perspective, this is fair enough. But it should not be the *sole* motivation of the Christian. A Christian must *in addition* focus on other *inputs*. I am not here referring to the process or resource inputs of the business, but to the *behavioural inputs of the Christian worker*. In other words, a Christian should set out to do the best he can, doing what is right before the Lord and leaving the outcome to the Lord. Let me illustrate this from history. When the Pilgrim fathers set up their new nation in America, they did not do so in order to become the most powerful and most prosperous nation on earth. They set themselves up to live their lives according to the light of their faith, doing the best they could in terms of 'inputs'. The outcome was the USA. So it should be when a new business is founded or new employment is taken. The primary goal should be to operate according to the biblical principles as developed in this book. Christians should see it as an opportunity to glorify God through evangelism, as already mentioned. The business outcomes *are* important as there is no point in going out of business because of poor business practices, but they are secondary to getting the 'inputs' correct. In the process, the business may do very well if God chooses to bless its endeavours. That, however, is a reward, not the motive.

We now develop what these inputs should be:

### DILIGENCE

We are to work *diligently*. However, we are also to work as if our 'employer' is God. Paul says we are to work 'heartily, *as for the Lord*' (Colossians 3:23, emphasis mine). (See also Ecclesiastes 9:10.) Surely, this makes a dramatic difference in our attitude to our employer or customer. Couple this with the realization that our main task at work is to glorify God and to point men and women to Christ. Our jobs then take on new meaning. We *will* become salt and light. Diligent work means applying all our faculties to the task that is entrusted to us, using all of the skills God has given us. It means working with a cheerful heart in which our attitudes and our actions are in unison. All of which is part of integrity. It means keeping our promises and meeting deadlines. It means not being asked twice to do something. In short, it means remembering that we are to work 'as for the Lord'. I know a cobbler who fixes shoes. When he returns the shoes to his customers, they look like new (sometimes better!). He charges a fair price and his customers marvel at his work.

When we commented on this, his response was something like this: 'When I started fixing shoes, I determined that I would work for God and not just my customer.' It shows.

Conscientious workers sometimes fall into the trap of believing that diligence means working long hours, sometimes on Saturday and even on a Sunday. I must confess to all of these mistakes.

Before proceeding, however, let us consider some history. In biblical times, a working week would have been twelve hours for six days. In Genesis chapter 1, it appears that God worked these hours. Are we expected to do that? Maybe in total, but a fair portion of this can be around the home, essentially with the family—even washing the dishes. This is all work. However, things have changed dramatically over the past hundred years. At no time in history have people worked so little and enjoyed so much 'leisure' time, nor have they spent so little time doing household chores such as cleaning, washing the dishes, etc. This is due to our labour saving machines. In Europe, a typical working week is a mere thirty-five (or fewer) hours. In our day, the pursuit of pleasure, laziness and general idleness are commonplace. The average British household now watches thirty-five hours of television a week. Nevertheless, many readers will complain of having no time to spare and very little for church, family or other noble causes. It is not unreasonable to conclude then that this group of people also have little time for the leisure pursuits mentioned above. How do we reconcile these two divergent positions? I suspect that many of the readers of this book are in employment that superficially demands more time than the standard thirty-five hours. The devil is good at making us sin by throwing us off balance and by causing us to go to an *excess* in the very thing at which we are trying to be good. Our work easily becomes idolatrous. In many arenas, we must maintain a balance between several truths—never between truth and error. With respect to time, the truth is: our first loyalty is to God. This means that our worship, whether it is private, family or public, gets priority. Then comes our family. *Discipline* and *self-control* are needed so as not to make our family suffer because we are at work too long. It is important to come home at an hour that will allow for time with the family, especially over the evening meal and family devotions. It is important, too, to be available over weekends to play sport with the family or to watch them if they are doing so, or maybe just to do things around the home in proximity to the family. Then comes our income earning work. Despite all that I have said about the workplace being a mission field, there is a limit to how much time should be spent there. You will probably be tied to agreed hours of work and these must be given unstintingly. There may also be the need to work a bit of overtime on occasions but getting into the routine practice of sacrificing your spiritual service and your family for your work should be avoided. Provided that you apply yourself wholeheartedly while at work and do what you are paid to do, perhaps a little more, you can leave work with a clear conscience. The principles underlying this subject are well developed in Mark Greene's book *Thank God it's Monday*.[1] Should I be more specific? A working week of around forty hours is not unreasonable and if this rises to fifty or even sixty occasionally, it should not ruin your spiritual life or your family. But regular seventy or even eighty hour weeks for your employer are to be avoided—even if you are self-employed. Your work is becoming an idol!

I know a family who created a family business which permitted the entire family to gather at breakfast, lunch and dinner so that they could read the Bible and pray together three times a day. They would not accept jobs which required long commuting times. This may not always be possible, but it is worth stopping to think about re-arranging your lifestyle. Holidays (though never mentioned in the Bible) are a blessing. It is common nowadays to enjoy four or even more weeks of vacation or holiday each year. Use them wisely.

All of the above is probably more aimed at men because they are usually the primary breadwinner and the worst offenders in this respect (although I acknowledge that it may apply to women as well). Many women will regard their primary work as that of a homemaker. All too often our assumption is that this means that the wife works twelve hours a day and 'lets the man off the hook'. Not at all. His *work* is also as homemaker, albeit with a different role. The husband and father is the head of the home and this is not only achieved by bringing in the money, but also by sharing in the *work* of building a home, of which bringing in the money is only one part.

### EXCELLENCE

Closely coupled to diligence is excellence. Can a Christian ever deliver mediocre work? Sadly, some might. But if we remember who our employer really is, will anything shoddy or incomplete ever be acceptable? We should not strive for excellence simply because this produces better profits (it does) or more customers (it will) or any other business outcome. We should strive for excellence because *we love God*. He sees what we do even when others do not. Working after hours to complete a task properly may not be noticed by anyone. It must, nevertheless, glorify God. 'So ... whatever you do, do all to the glory of God' (1 Corinthians 10:31).

### MOTIVATION

In the next chapter we shall be considering a behavioural view of motivation which is based on man's need to satisfy a hierarchy of needs (Maslow[2]). This is, in part at least, reasonable and, perhaps, a discovery of a natural law. But is the highest level of motivation what Maslow calls 'self-actualization'? This conveys a selfish attitude and does not fit into a biblical framework. The Bible offers another, far stronger motivation for a Christian worker—*love*. Love has many forms and the particular love that applies here is not sentimental love, nor brotherly love, nor erotic love but self-sacrificing love, *agape* in the Greek. The thrust of *agape* is that it seeks to benefit the *recipient* and not the giver. It always seeks the best for the person being loved. Jesus defined it well when he said, 'Greater love [*agape*] has no one than this, that someone lays down his life for his friends' (John 15:13).

The Bible teaches us that we should be motivated by *love*—firstly, for Christ. This is surely very countercultural. Most of us are probably motivated by the possibility of a bonus! We shall deal with the subject more fully in the next chapter, but consider what the Bible says, 'Whatever you do, work heartily, as for the Lord and not for men, knowing that from the Lord you will receive the inheritance as *your reward. You are serving the Lord Christ*' (Colossians 3:23–24, emphasis mine). Paul is saying that we must see the 'Lord Christ' as the one for whom we work and not our employer! Do you work well, not for satisfying an earthly need, but for Jesus' sake? In case anyone is tempted to think that this is an isolated verse, let me cite another example. In the parallel passage in Ephesians, Paul, writing to slaves, gave these instructions: 'Slaves, obey your earthly masters with fear and trembling, with a sincere heart, as you would Christ, not by the way of eye-service, as people-pleasers, but as *servants of Christ*, doing the will of God from the heart, rendering service with a good will *as to the Lord* and not to man, knowing that whatever good anyone does, this he will receive back from the Lord, whether he is a slave or free' (Ephesians 6:5–8, emphasis mine). The masters referred to here were in all probability pagan Romans who may have been harsh and unkind. Notice that the slaves' ultimate reward would come from God, hence the encouragement to work 'as to the Lord'. We should keep this in mind when we find ourselves in unhappy work situations, especially when the person to whom we are accountable is difficult.

This concept of *agape* goes further. It should be the motivation for all *service*. We should *serve* our customers, patients, students, even colleagues with *agape* love. Put simply, we should seek to do things for *their* benefit. Consider a salesman offering something to a customer. If he puts the customer first, then he will seek to offer the product or service which is *best for the customer*, not for his own commission or even the company's profit. A good teacher will do everything possible to help a student learn and a good doctor will seek to maximize the patient's comfort and return to health, not his own income. A lot of this will be endorsed by the professions as good ethical behaviour, but I am going further. I am saying that the *motivating force* in rendering any service should be *agape* love.

One aspect of incentives and rewards needs special mention, namely, that of greed. A fine line exists between greed on the one hand, doing the best job possible on the other, and being rewarded by an appreciative employer. The difference lies largely in our attitude before and while we are working. Why did we do a good job? Was it merely to get a bonus? The true motive will soon be discovered if an outstanding job is done but nothing extra is rewarded for the effort. Does the employee feel aggrieved or does the person continue to be motivated to do his best? Is pursuing wealth a passion? Is it, perhaps, the number one passion? If it is, then God has been replaced by wealth and that is idolatry. The free enterprise system provides many temptations and the scope to satisfy them. None is more serious than satisfying greed. We need constantly to pray for deliverance and for the grace to control our desires. For a more detailed look at this subject, read *Beyond Greed* by Brian Rosner.[3]

### INTEGRITY

Integrity is often considered the hallmark of a Christian in business. What does it mean? The word occurs at least twenty-five times in the Bible and often in conjunction with the phrase or words 'good faith', 'righteousness' and 'uprightness'. Here is a typical verse: 'If you will walk before me, as David your father walked, with integrity of heart and uprightness, doing according to all that I have commanded you, and keeping my statutes and my rules…' (1 Kings 9:4). The word conveys the idea of 'completeness'. Completeness in what? From the above verse it is clear that we are to be complete in keeping God's moral law, both in the heart—that is, in our attitude, and in our actions. It means keeping *every* point of the law. Being *consistent* in applying the truth to everything that we do. Clearly, this means upholding all of God's laws. James goes even further when he says, 'So whoever knows the right thing to do and *fails to do it*, for him it is sin' (James 4:17, emphasis mine). James is saying that even if we *fail* to act and remain silent when we should have done or said something, we are guilty of sin. Remember how Daniel was described with regard to his service for a heathen kingdom: 'They could find no ground for complaint or any fault, because he [Daniel] was faithful, and no error or fault was found in him' (Daniel 6:4). The *NIV* uses the words 'neither corrupt nor negligent'. Notice the terms that describe Daniel: 'no fault', 'faithful', 'no error', 'nor negligent'. He was guilty of no sin of commission *nor* sin of omission. In a word, Daniel acted with integrity.

Integrity means doing what is morally right, not just what is contained in an agreement. A fine example of this comes from the founder of the Heinz organization (the 57 varieties man). He went bankrupt but carefully noted to whom he owed money and when he had recovered, he settled every debt. The worst example in my own experience occurred in

Australia. We had a so-called shareholder's agreement with a partner which regulated our relationship. When things started to change, our partners simply moved in a particular direction to suit themselves. When I politely pointed out that this was not in accordance with the agreement, the response was along these lines: 'Don't lecture me on legal matters. This is not a legal issue but a negotiating position. It depends on how deep your pockets are and how much time you have.' No doubt this was reality but not the kind of ethics that should be practised by any Christian.

### CONFLICT OF INTEREST

A subtle but important application of integrity lies in avoiding conflicts of interest. This arises when a person uses his position to advance his own interest or that of someone or some entity close to that person. It is generally illegal and directors who infringe conflict rules are committing an offence. But what about in lower ranks? All of us should be on the look out for potential conflicts and advance no cause other than that of the business for which we are working. Let me illustrate. Imagine a company that wishes to change its supplier of a critical service where the present supplier is the son of one of the directors. Everyone will naturally become sensitive about making any change. What should happen? The father should excuse himself from any meetings that discusses this subject and make it clear that he will respect and support any decision made in the best interests *of the company* and not in the best interests of his son. That is not only the *legal* duty of the director but also the *moral* duty. There must be no conflicting motives in anything that is done for an employer. If in doubt, the potential conflict should always be declared. Remember Daniel, who was neither 'corrupt nor negligent', and he was working for an evil pagan state.

### BRIBERY

Integrity can be compromised in the giving and receiving of gifts. In many parts of the world, bribery is a standard way of life. While we may qualitatively understand the difference between a 'gift' and a bribe, in practice there must be a line somewhere that marks the difference. This line will be different for everyone and it is necessary to think through some of the issues raised in this section. Various studies have produced corruption indices (or the opposite which is a transparency index). One such list, known as The Transparency International Corruption Perceptions Index,[4] produces no surprises. Western Europe, North America, Australia and New Zealand (and many other countries outside of my experience) maintain relatively high standards and hence readers from these countries may not fully appreciate the problem. The tightest rules that I ever encountered were in Australia. I once paid a courtesy call on a government official from whom we had purchased technology. The afternoon coffee cart came around but the official refused to offer me any. Instead, he asked me to accompany him to the canteen where we each paid for our own coffee. This seems extreme, but is certainly keeping on the safe side. On the other hand, one of the most blatant attempts to extract a gift from our company occurred in the USA. Human nature is not bound by geography! Where do we draw the line? Clearly, a cup of coffee for the chief executive is never going to be a bribe. But, perhaps, giving a lower-ranked employee a gourmet lunch may well affect his judgement. If a company is prepared to apply a variable standard, then it can define an allowable benefit in terms of a person's salary. If any form of benefit, such as a lunch or dinner, is limited to 0·1 per cent (for argument's sake) of a person's monthly income, then the chief executive earning £10,000 per month would be able to accept a lunch worth £10. This is unlikely to be a bribe to such a person. The acceptance of obvious advertising handouts such as pens, calendars, diaries and the like can also be permitted. It is important to determine whether or not the gift is likely to affect a person's judgement or simply keep the company name before the customer—the object of all advertising. On the other hand, if the decision is taken to maintain the same standard for everyone, then a low value can be set which rules everyone out of temptation. In our company, we applied another strict rule to cover the situation where a meeting with a potential client took place over a meal. The meal would have to be simple, either served in the canteen or sandwiches in the conference room—no gourmet lunch in a restaurant!

A more complex problem arises when there is the suspicion that in some parts of the world business will be lost or won through bribes. As a company, either you do not accept business in that country or you work around the problem the usual way by appointing an agent who gets a commission with which you leave him to do whatever he wishes. I am uncomfortable with this route if the commission is larger than would normally be paid for the services rendered and if some of the commission is very likely to be routed to the customer. From experience I know that in some countries, known for their corruption, commissions can be as high as ninety per cent. Clearly, this is unacceptable as it is not difficult to guess where much of the money goes. While writing this book, one of our companies was faced with precisely this problem. I am pleased to say that our directors rejected the offer to win a very large order based on what really was a thinly disguised bribe of this type. I am also happy to say that the biggest single order I ever won was in Malaysia (not high on the transparency lists). At no time during the negotiations, nor during the contract, did the customer ever allow me to pay for a meal or even a cup of coffee; he always paid.

Any form of bribery or corruption is categorically condemned in the Bible. To quote from just two verses: 'For I know how many are your transgressions and how great are your sins—you who afflict the righteous, *who take a bribe*' (Amos 5:12, emphasis mine). We need to remember once again Daniel who was 'neither corrupt not negligent' (Daniel 6:4, *NIV*).

One would expect that all this is obvious to every Christian in paid employment. Sadly, that is not my experience. In fact, if I discovered that a job applicant was a Christian, I was especially cautious. I sometimes found that the Christians at work were less upright and less honest than many non-Christians. (However, I am grateful to say that this was not always true.) I know many colleagues who live upright lives, observe the work ethic and portray great integrity but make no profession of being Christians.

The business world is aware that rules governing ethics and behaviour are necessary. Consequently, over the years governments have passed laws regulating the behaviour of companies and their office bearers. However, business itself has not been satisfied even with the strictest laws. Over the past few decades business, industry and the stock exchanges have set up special 'governance' committees defining very specific rules covering disclosure, reporting, behaviour of office bearers, auditors, stockbrokers, etc. Basically, business has recognized the need to control sinful mankind!

Christians, on the other hand, believe that they are saved from sin. This is correct. Some then erroneously believe that they *automatically* live a new life which is victorious over sin. They do their jobs without any *proactive* effort to suppress their natural tendency to sin. They assume that they will naturally tell the truth. They fail to understand that Christians are called upon to *walk carefully* (Ephesians 5:15 and following) because it is *not natural to be free from sin*. Our natural tendency is to sin as Paul said so clearly, 'For we know that the law is spiritual, but I am of the flesh, sold under sin. I do not understand my own actions. For I do not do what I want, but *I do the very thing I hate*' (Romans 7:14–15, emphasis mine). If Paul recognized that he did the very things that he hated, how much more do we succumb? We can never simply assume that we will be different. For example, it takes *effort* to tell the truth in the sense that we convey an accurate and precise account of all that we communicate. Certainly, James considered this to be a problem, and so do I! See what James has to say, 'For we all *stumble in many ways*, and if anyone does not stumble in what *he says*, he is a perfect man, able also to bridle his whole body' (James 3:2, emphasis mine). He went on to say, 'But above all, my brothers, do not swear, either by heaven or by earth or by any other oath, but let your "yes" be yes and your "no" be no' (James 5:12). Every time we speak, we should check what we are about to say *before* we open our mouths. Or, if what has been said is not accurate, withdraw it immediately. This is an application of self-control which is commended by Paul: 'But the fruit of the Spirit is … self-control; against such things there is no law' (Galatians 5:22–23).

We now turn to some further examples of how integrity should affect the way we conduct ourselves at work.

### 'YOU SHALL NOT STEAL'

Naturally, a Christian may not steal anything from his employer: not his time, his pencils, his telephone, his postage stamps, nor his stationery, and so the list could go on. But many do! Many employers, for example, accept that it is efficient for an employee to use the company phone to do some 'private business'. But this must be checked first, otherwise, it is stealing. If it is allowed, integrity needs to be shown by keeping the costs to a minimum. On the other hand, employees could take their private mobile phones to work. One's own stationery should be brought to the office as well as one's own postage stamps. Never use company time or take time off without permission.

During my periods of being at the head of various organizations, I was frequently approached to support charities or Christian organizations. The underlying assumption was that as a Christian I would be sympathetic to the cause and readily give company funds. But is this ethical? My shareholders expected me to be a faithful steward of *their* funds. It was not my money to give away; nor could I use my work time unwisely to further the gospel or any charity. Faithfulness and good stewardship called on me to devote my work time to serving the company and the shareholders' interests. That is what I was paid to do. One way out of this dilemma is to give a personal contribution or agree to publicize the need in the company and let individuals contribute as they wish to.

Our companies are sometimes asked by Christian organizations to do work for nothing or at a reduced cost. Our companies all have minority shareholders so that all of the resources and assets in the company belong in part to them. It would be stealing to force them to give up some of their income to any cause, however good it may be. What is the answer? Give the organization a donation to permit them to pay the full price or pay the difference out of your own pocket. *Integrity may not come free.*

Theft is taking or using anything from someone else without permission. The 'anything' means any property, moveable, immovable or intellectual. Do we ignore copyright? Do we illegally copy software? I trust not. Every Christian worker should go through his software every so often and check to see that it is all legal.

### STEWARDSHIP AND FAITHFULNESS

Jesus commended *faithfulness* (or trustworthiness) in the parable of the faithful servant who used the talents entrusted to him to fulfil his owner's best interest: 'His master said to him, "Well done, good and faithful servant. You have been faithful over a little; I will set you over much. Enter into the joy of your master"' (Matthew 25:21). Paul stated plainly: 'Moreover, it is required of stewards that they be found trustworthy' (1 Corinthians 4:2). Faithfulness includes trustworthiness which in turn demands commitment. Our present secular culture finds little virtue in commitment or stewardship. Few employees care about what happens to the company or its customers. This is why strikes happen so easily. In 2004 I was appalled to hear that the British Airways check-in staff at Heathrow Airport simply walked off the job, sometimes in the middle of checking in a passenger. It was an unofficial strike and without warning. Whatever the merits of the case may have been, what was completely lacking was any commitment to British Airways or to the passengers. The ensuing chaos at Heathrow and the knock-on effect throughout the world was not considered. What surprised me even more was that I did not hear a single commentator mentioning the morality of this action, or the manifest lack of commitment. Our secular culture simply assumes that these virtues do not matter and upholds the 'rights' of the check-in staff to do as they please, regardless of the consequences. This is a typical case where a Christian world view will be diametrically opposite to the prevailing secular world view.

We must also observe and implement the fundamental rules and practices of whatever form of employment we are in. We need to be exemplary in the way we equip ourselves to do a good job. I know of a group of well-meaning Christians who founded a business that was meant to do great things for the Lord. Within two months of commencing operations, it had gone bankrupt with considerable loss to shareholders. The founders had not taken care to implement sound business practices. There is no witness nor value in such a venture! Imagine that there is a person who is very anxious to help sick people and glorify God by his care and concern for them. So, that person simply sets himself up as a doctor. No, it is necessary to go through long and arduous training before one can do the work of a doctor. So it is with almost all jobs, perhaps not as long, but one needs to learn how to do the work *well*. This is glorifying to God.

Please notice that nowhere in any of the passages dealing with work is anyone commended for the position or the grade that he attains. There are no 'big jobs' or 'little jobs'—only faithfully done jobs. It does not matter if you are the cleaner or the chairman. You glorify God by how you do the job. When we lived in South Africa, my wife and I enjoyed the friendship of a black African couple. The husband was once a drunkard but had been converted through street evangelism. He and his wife developed into a truly godly couple who played a significant role in their church. His income earning job was as a messenger at the South African Mint and his wife cleaned the toilets. They were excited about the work they did and spoke warmly of the contribution they could make as Christians in these roles. They were good stewards. We came to love them dearly and also to respect them.

## SUBMISSION

The times we live in emphasize our 'rights'. Our culture does not like authority. Submission (or its near cousin, obedience) to a superior at work is seen as 'old fashioned'. Employees believe that they have the right to do as they please. Yet the Bible is full of submission. First and foremost, we are all to submit to Christ and to his Word (Romans 8:7; 10:3; James 4:7). The command to submit, however, is to *all* in authority. Note Paul's basis for teaching submission: 'Let every person be subject to the governing authorities. For there is no authority except from God, and those that exist have been instituted by God. Therefore whoever resists the authorities resists what God has appointed, and those who resist will incur judgement' (Romans 13:1–2). This passage is usually interpreted with respect to the political authority. But does it not say that there is no authority except from God? Paul makes this clear when he applies it to slaves: 'Slaves, obey your earthly masters with fear and trembling, with a sincere heart, as you would Christ' (Ephesians 6:5). We must apply this to our attitude to our earthly employers as well. Submission does not mean that employees do what they say only when they agree with them. It means that they do what their superiors say *when they do not agree*. Naturally, they should have the right, even the duty, to point out to the person to whom they report if he is about to make a mistake, but in the end employees must submit. This will be glorifying to God because we should do so 'as [we] would [obey] Christ'. (See Ephesians 6:5 cited above.)

**TIME MANAGEMENT**

One of the most valuable assets that you own and, in essence, sell to your employer (or to your customer if you are self-employed) is your time. It is, therefore, essential that you exercise good stewardship in the way you use your time. You are stealing if you do your own private business, or the work of the church or even evangelism in the time that you have sold. Equally, you are defrauding your employer if you are *negligent* in the way you use time. We have already established that a sin of omission is as serious as a sin of commission. (See James 4:17.)

The Christian faith uniquely teaches that time is 'linear'—that is, it began in eternity (or infinity) past and then moves in a linear fashion through our world and on into a future eternity. In this context, our period on earth is extremely short. We are, therefore, called upon to make the most of our time, to be good stewards of this wasting asset. Paul gives this instruction to both the Ephesians and to the Colossians. He tells them to '[make] the best use of the time, because the days are evil' (Ephesians 5:16).

The subject of time management is both important and detailed. The scope of this book does not permit me to say much apart from a few general points. I have included a worksheet in the Annexure for those who wish to monitor their present use of time.

A common refrain is 'I don't have enough time.' We marvel at others who get a great deal done while we are constantly struggling to get *anything* done. We are probably perturbed by the many balls that we drop as we attempt to juggle all of the conflicting requirements on our time.

What is the solution?

In a nutshell, we have to be proactive in the way we organize our lives. Here are a few practical tips which are more appropriate for office-type work:

1. First of all, make sure you only do that which needs to be done. The greatest enemy to our time is doing things which either should not be

done at all or can be done by someone else. Eliminate all trivia, unnecessary reading or TV watching and ration your recreation to that which is helpful. I remember when I left university with my first degree, our professor gave us three pieces of advice to help us succeed in life. The advice was: marry a good wife (I agreed and did); learn how to mix drinks because this will give you social skills which are essential (I spent forty years in business proving this one wrong); and play golf. I enjoy golf and played a lot of it at university (much more than any of my fellow players!) but once I started working, I simply could not find the time. Wrong again! My wife and I played tennis until our boys had left home *because it took less time*. I have nothing against golf, but it was a sacrifice I had to make. You may have to make other sacrifices.

2. Make sure you are applying the correct amount of effort to whatever you do. It is tempting to be a perfectionist and never get anything finished. I am not contradicting my point about excellence, merely suggesting that the correct level of quality must be found for every task.

Thereafter *focus* your time into achieving *outcomes*. Most people are unfocused and wander aimlessly around the multitude of tasks that come their way. They do not prioritize issues, have no timetable for their day and usually end up wasting time fretting about unfinished work which they eventually put into a 'pending file' of some sort. Does this sound familiar?

One antidote for this is to plan the next day every evening before you leave work. Jot down what you want to *complete* the next day and try to group all your activities into time slots. Some of these time slots will be filled already because you will no doubt have appointments or time deadlines already on your calendar. *Remember to drop those things which should not be done at all.*

Set the first half-hour of every day to do all the small, and perhaps low priority, items, clearing them out while your mind is still fresh and before you really get into the day. You are probably surprised that I recommend doing the low priority items first. Yes, that is correct. If you do not 'knock them off the list' immediately, they will never get done! As you complete each allotted task, take great delight in physically crossing it off your list. You will be amazed at how quickly you get things done and how little you fret when you feel that everything is taken care of and that you are in control of your time. Background fretting is one of the major reasons for low output at work.

3. Whenever something comes across your desk, you can take one of four actions:
   - **Do it**. Deal with it immediately or add it to the list of what you will do in that first half-hour on the next day.
   - **Dump it**. Decide not to do anything about it and put it into the bin.
   - **Delegate it**. If others are capable of doing the work (even your superiors), then delegate it to them. Remember to ask them to report back so that you can check that it has been done. (This is part of management control dealt with in the next chapter.)
   - **Defer it**. This is a last resort and should not rise above five per cent of all activities that come your way. It is usually a way of avoiding having to make a decision, but you mentally justify your inaction by telling yourself that it is not an urgent matter anyway. Probably true, but once you defer something, you will spend a great deal of unnecessary time picking up the pieces when you do eventually get around to doing it. Wasted time is not good stewardship.

If you are in manual work, you should ensure that you organize your work well, taking care to do the following:
- Have all the necessary tools and materials readily available before you start.
- Have tools which make the task as efficient as possible. As your time is costly to your company or your customer, you should work as quickly as possible.
- Do not take all the breaks that you are 'entitled to', but try to combine various types of breaks.
- Plan and organize your work beforehand so that you get it done effectively and efficiently.
- Remember to do the work to the correct standard. Poor workmanship is cheating your customer. It is also possible to overdo the standard and waste time.

- Commit to a completion time and work hard to achieve it. It becomes a self-fulfilling prophecy.

In Annexure B the worksheet shows how to increase your time available for work. This may be the most important aspect of time management.

### AMBITION

James condemns *selfish ambition*. Ambition is fine when it is to do the best that a person can. But *selfish ambition* is not to be condoned. Read what James has to say: 'But if you have bitter jealousy and *selfish ambition* in your hearts ... This is not the wisdom that comes down from above, but is earthly, unspiritual, demonic. For where jealousy and *selfish ambition* exist, there will be disorder and every vile practice' (James 3:14–16, emphasis mine). Once again, Christians must follow a culture which is completely contrary to the prevailing secular one. If our real goal at work is to glorify God through our life and testimony, then we should stop being ambitious simply in order to advance. May I give a personal word of testimony. In reflecting on my own career, as far as I can recall, I only once applied for a job or a promotion in seven job movements. Positions were offered to me, often 'out of the blue'. My policy of leaving the results to the Lord did *me* no harm. However, I acknowledge that this may not always be true.

Jesus made an interesting response to the mother of James and John who wanted her sons to be the greatest in Christ's kingdom. Jesus did not reject the request. Rather he said, 'But whoever would be great among you must be your servant ...' (Matthew 20:26). Being ambitious or wanting to be 'great' is fine, but greatness in God's kingdom is to be found in being a servant. Our ambition should be to *serve*.

### SELLING

Many readers will be involved in the selling process, either as sales people or in management where selling is a major component of the job. This is inevitable in a free market economy. Perhaps in this role we need to exercise the most care as to 'how we walk' and how we apply all of the abovementioned principles. We shall focus on just three principles which will be especially relevant to selling.

The first concern in selling is to be absolutely truthful. This does not mean that we have to tell the potential customer everything that we know about the company, the product, its manufacture and its costing (warts and all). Trying to do so could demean people or infringe patents, copyright or confidential information. It may also be tedious, boring and quite simply unnecessary! What *is* necessary is that we tell him all that he *needs to know* as a potential buyer. The information must be absolutely true and clear. This may cause a dilemma. What if you know that your products or services are below standard or overpriced? Can you, in good conscience, sell them? Are you in a situation where you know that if you give the potential customer your honest opinion, you will not sell a thing? If this is the case, you will fail as a salesperson and the dilemma will be over for you because you will soon be looking for another job. So, short circuit the process and look for another job as soon as you come to the conclusion that you cannot sell the products or service with good conscience. However, I am not suggesting that you can only sell 'Rolls Royce' products. Consider the following diagram:

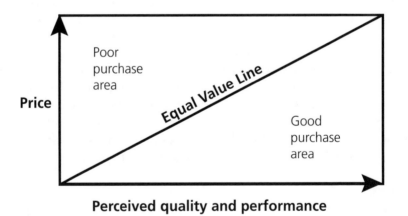

**Perceived quality and performance**

Not all products are of equal quality, nor do all products cost the same price. This is fine and just what is to be expected in a free market. Provided that the price and the quality bear a direct relationship to each other, the purchaser is buying 'equal value'. Put differently, if a product of a certain quality and performance costs £1 and another which is twice as good costs £2, then both are good or equal in value. Not all low-priced products are bad value and not all highly-priced products are good value. Indeed, one of the tricks of marketing is to sell high-priced goods which *do not offer* correspondingly higher quality or performance. They are overpriced and are to be found in the left hand triangle of the diagram. Products which offer good quality or performance, but cost relatively less, lie within the right hand triangle.

No Christian should be selling (or buying) in the left hand triangle. Provided that he is selling in the right hand triangle, a salesperson can explain to a customer that his product may not be the best available, nor the lowest priced, but that it is *good value* for money. If it lies well below the equal value line, he is selling a bargain! This is the integrity that must be demonstrated by every Christian salesperson. In my experience, it nearly always results in success as well!

The second quality that a Christian salesperson must demonstrate is (*agape*) love for his customer. He must be so concerned about the customer's best interest that he makes sure that the customer gets what is best *for him*, even if this means earning less commission and reducing the company profits in the process. The salesperson must also demonstrate real concern for the customer. I always include my home and mobile telephone numbers on my business cards and my customers know that I am available to them '24/7'. Once again, such selling will often produce the best results.

Finally, a Christian salesperson must not be motivated by greed. As we show elsewhere, being rewarded for a good job through commission or a bonus is legitimate, but being *driven* by greed will quickly sacrifice the principles mentioned above and will damage that person's own soul.

All of the above applies, even if used cars or insurance are being sold!

### EVANGELISM

Have you worked out what all this is pointing to? It is telling us that work to the glory of God results in evangelism. Christ is most glorified at the cross! Surely, this is true of every aspect of our lives. We are to point men and women to Christ. Work is just one special kind of evangelism and our workplace one special mission field. It is not just speaking to our fellow workmates, although it will include this. As I have stated earlier, on this latter subject, be careful not to steal your employer's time to speak to your colleagues. The biggest impact will be by *living* your life in a special way, so that God is glorified. I know an alcoholic who was so impressed by the life of a colleague that he eventually came to Christ and is now a full-time street evangelist. Actions generally speak louder than words.

Why is this so important? Churches and missions quite rightly go to great lengths to reach out to neighbours and others through evangelistic efforts. In the secular world, this is very hard work. And, yet, every Christian at work is in contact with unbelievers every day. The chances are that the ratio of Christians to non-Christians in your place of employment is comparable with that of Saudi Arabia! Here is the greatest cross-cultural mission field right around you every day. In fact, you will probably spend more time with non-Christians than you will with your spouse. But even more important, your work colleagues cannot ignore your message if it is preached from your *life* rather than your *lips*.

Mark Greene, in his excellent book, *Thank God it's Monday,*[5] deals with this subject extensively in an easy-to-read, humorous and yet profound way. I shall quote just one paragraph:

Importantly, in the workplace the witness comes in a form that cannot be tuned out like a radio programme, zapped like a television broadcast, thrown away like a tract or turned down like an invitation to the concert. The non-Christian can tune out almost every form of the gospel, but he cannot—short of murder or Machiavellian office politics—tune out the spectacle of the Christian living in the power of the spirit day by day, hour by hour, crisis by crisis.

## Summary of chapter 2

We have seen that a Christian world view is often diametrically opposed to the secular world view of our age. A Christian culture acknowledges the dual nature of mankind, namely, human beings are made in God's image but have fallen into sin. It stresses a behaviour based on diligent work, integrity, responsibility, stewardship, faithfulness, submission, commitment, working out of love for the Lord and rejects stealing, bribery, one-sided rights, entitlement, selfish ambition and handouts.

The overarching goal of all Christians at work must be to glorify God by pointing men and women to Christ though their lives and their testimonies.

## Case studies

### CASE STUDY 1

Early in my career I heard of an outstanding case of integrity. I worked for a steel company which sold substandard steel products to employees at the price of scrap (which it really was). Some of the directors of the company owned farms and needed large quantities of fencing wire. As the company operated a modern and efficient wire plant, very little wire scrap was generated and yet our general manager was under pressure to deliver scrap wire to the directors. He was in a difficult position. If he did not deliver the wire, he thought that he would be in trouble with the directors and yet he refused to reclassify good material as scrap. So, what did he do? It could be argued that he should have simply refused and, if put under overt pressure, he should have reported a conspiracy to commit fraud. The problem was that everyone would have denied it and he could have been victimized without being able to do anything about it. He preferred to 'heap coals of fire on the heads' of the people involved. He shipped the good material, paid for it himself and recovered the scrap value from the director. His integrity cost him dearly. While we operate in a secular world with low ethics, *we will sometimes have to pay the price of our world view.*

**CASE STUDY 2**

Every business that buys or sells over a scale must conform to laws which require the scales to be checked (assized) by government inspectors. They will allow a certain degree of inaccuracy, for example, + or −0·1 per cent error.

I worked for many years in the metals industry. Raw materials and the finished goods are mostly bought and sold by weight. Many large reputable businesses will need several scales and, generally, everyone accepts that sometimes the scales will read a little high and, at other times, a bit low. This is in the nature of the technology and within the legal limits. A good deal of the raw materials was scrap metal which is a very valuable commodity. The methods of cheating by the suppliers are legion. Here are a few examples: the truck carrying the scrap metal is weighed on entering the works. While the metal is being offloaded, the driver will 'clean' the truck, tidying up the cab and throwing out a heap of rubbish. He will empty his coffee flask and drain some water from a mysterious tank and so forth. When he leaves the works, he will then have the empty truck weighed again and the difference between the two weights will theoretically be the weight of scrap metal delivered. Not quite! What he left in the works included the weight of all the other (non metal) items that he disposed of while he was offloading!

The industry response to this and other malpractices has been to introduce a legal correction. Most processing works will have two scales: one which is used to buy metal and set at the 'minus' inaccuracy allowed so that the works always pays for a bit less than what is delivered. The other scale will be used for selling and this will be set at the 'plus' inaccuracy so that customers pay for a little more than what they get. Amos had harsh words for those who 'deal deceitfully with false balances' (Amos 8:5). See also Deuteronomy 25:13–16.

## Discussion

The practice of buying and selling over two different scales is perfectly within the law. Consider the financial results. If a works buys £50 million a year of scrap and the scales are set 0·1 per cent low, then the works gains £50,000 a year. This same works would sell about £100 million worth of finished goods, and if the 'selling scale' is set 0·1 per cent high, then the extra income would be £100,000 a year. So, a total increase in profit of £150,000 a year can be made. Is this practice morally justified?

When I was running a copper and brass works, I would not allow the use of two scales. I insisted that the scales be set as accurately as possible and, to prove our good faith, we bought and sold over the same scale.

## Discussion questions

1. While the practice described above is not illegal, why do you think it should not be practised? Which biblical references would you use to justify your answer?
2. How does the 'dual nature of man' differ from secular thinking?
3. Can you list ways which are, perhaps, not obvious but which fail to meet biblical standards of integrity at work?
4. Does 'diligent work' mean working long hours? What is reasonable in your view?
5. Can you think of any time when your Christian views have resulted in some cost to you?
6. In the notes at the end of the book, I have included a 'Code of ethics'. This is a generic form of one that we have devised together with our staff and which we encourage all companies to adopt. Get together with other Christians in your workplace and adapt this for your work situation. Present it to your employer and, even if he does not want to adopt it, why not get all the Christians to adopt it in the way they work. You need not tell your employer, *he should notice*!

# Managing People

Many readers will have reached some sort of management position, or at least be moving towards such a position. Management theory is freely available and taught in the business schools. Your company may even offer internal training or sponsor you to pursue a course of study on 'management' at some college. I certainly enjoyed these privileges, even though I came to differ with some aspects of what was being taught on how to manage people. The question for the Christian to answer is whether or not he should follow secular theories or look to the Bible for guidance. Paul put it this way: 'Do I make my plans *according to the flesh*, ready to say "Yes, yes" and "No, no" at the same time?' (2 Corinthians 1:17, emphasis mine). A fair proportion of management theory is 'natural law' and is, therefore, legitimate. But we need to be on our guard to make sure that we are not drawn into behaviour which is unbiblical.

A Christian manager faces an additional dilemma. Firstly, he will probably have to manage people who are functioning according to a secular world view and who will probably not share the views that I have been presenting. Secondly, he is obliged to manage according to his own Christian world view which will be rather different from what his employer and employees expect. There is no easy answer, but good example and patient coaching will go a long way towards convincing one's subordinates at least to hear one's case. Once during my career, a subordinate simply could not accept my views. He even stated that integrity was a luxury that no executive could afford. In time, he realized that he did not fit in and resigned.

We shall step back initially and define some terms. What is management? Many definitions exist but most can be reduced to something along these lines: getting results through people or achieving outcomes through others. It deals with getting one's subordinates to *implement* objectives or tasks that may originate from any source. Usually tasks and even instructions come from outside of the business unit and the job of the manager is to get them done.

In classical theory, the elements of management are *planning, organizing, leading* and *controlling*. That will suffice for our purposes, although different schools will divide the tasks up differently. Each of these elements can be found in the Bible. Consequently, we can accept that this is another example of natural law that has been 'discovered' by management scientists, just as Newton discovered the law of gravity.

We shall examine each element of management and consider if it is concordant with biblical principles:

## Planning

Planning is not commanded in the Bible but Jesus simply assumed it in his illustration when he said, 'For which of you, desiring to build a tower, does not first sit down and count the cost, whether he has enough to complete it? … Or what king, going out to encounter another king in war, will not sit down first and deliberate whether he is able with ten thousand to meet him who comes against him with twenty thousand?' (Luke 14:28–31). Planning is ensuring that the future is managed in such a way that the specified goal is achieved. As Christians, we have a restraint. We are never to overlook the sovereignty of God. We may plan all we like but God will always have the last word (James 4:15).

## Organization

Organization occurs in one of the earliest recorded pieces of management advice. It came from Jethro, Moses' father-in-law.

When Moses' father-in-law saw all that he was doing for the people, he said, 'What is this that you are doing for the people? … What you are doing is not good. You and the people with you will certainly wear yourselves out, for the thing is too heavy for you. You are not able to do it alone. Now obey my voice; I will give you advice, and God be with you! You shall represent the people before God and bring their cases to God, and you shall warn them about the statutes and the laws, and make them know the way in which they must walk and what they must do. Moreover, look for able men from all the people, men who fear God, who are trustworthy and hate a bribe, and place such men over the people as chiefs of thousands, of hundreds, of fifties, and of tens. And let them judge the people at all times. Every great matter they shall bring to you, but any small matter they shall decide themselves. So it will be easier for you, and they will bear the burden with you. If you do this, God will direct you, you will be able to endure, and all this people also will go to their place in peace' (Exodus 18:14–23).

This was a political and judicial situation but the solution is valid in a business as well. Notice the steps: separation and classification of functions (what Adam Smith called 'division of labour'); identification of people with the correct skills (or gifts) and possessing integrity; delegation and a process whereby a problem could move up the chain of authority to be solved at the appropriate level. Notice, too, that Jethro advised Moses that everyone should know *what was expected of him*. A manager must ensure that every subordinate has goals and understands his role. This is a key principle in management.

## Leading
Leading in management is only a component of the broader subject of leadership, discussed more fully in the next chapter. In the context of management, it deals with leading subordinates to implement decisions, ensuring that staff know what they must accomplish and motivating them to perform.

## Controlling
A biblical understanding of the *sinfulness of man* must affect the way we manage people. People cannot be fully trusted because they are sinful and, therefore, must be controlled. At all times, people must be held accountable and operate within pre-established controls. The limits of the controls will be set in the first place in accordance with a person's seniority, but more particularly by his record of how well he has used whatever scope has been given in the past. We shall consider this in more detail.

One of the primary tasks of managers is to delegate authority to subordinates. Despite it being established in antiquity, the concept is one of the worst understood in management. It flows from the humanistic idea that people are intrinsically good and that they need self-actualization. This often results in subordinates wanting to be given some very broad boundaries and then to be left alone to do as they please within these boundaries, and even exceed the boundaries from time to time. This is a false view and is actually 'abdication'. Delegation must be achieved within the framework of a 'closed loop'. Let me explain. At the time that a manager delegates authority to a subordinate, he sets up a method of measuring the outcomes of the employee's actions compared to some predetermined objectives. Every week (or month, or quarter), the employee must account for what he has achieved. This usually comes from the management accounting system. If he fails to meet the objectives, then the manager will take some appropriate corrective action. This is known as the 'closed loop'. Every chief executive of every listed company knows this only too well because he has to report (in writing) to the shareholders at the end of every quarter or every six months. Auditors have to check all of the accounts and report independently that all is as stated. The world is fully aware of the need to call senior management to account and to check what is reported. This principle should be true even at the lowest level, with the reporting cycle being shorter the lower one goes. This principle is taught in conservative management books but, generally, it cuts across the assumptions held by secular thinkers and many employees.

The book of Nehemiah is a good example of a manager who practised all of the activities mentioned above.

## Secular world view

As we have already stated, we need to understand how people function if we are to manage them successfully. This, in turn, will be based on our assumptions about their behaviour. In western society, a great deal of management theory is based on a secular view which in turn is based on a number of underlying philosophies.

Another reason to understand the secular world view of our fellow human beings is so that we may evangelize them effectively. If a person were called to evangelize the Zulus for example, then, unless that person were a Zulu, he would study the Zulu culture or world view. Likewise, we must understand our secular colleagues who are the products of the philosophies briefly described below (with apologies to all philosophers):

## Secular humanism

It is difficult to summarize humanism partly because it has many divisions, including 'religious humanism'. Humanists issued three manifestos in the twentieth century, each with a different emphasis, complicating our task of understanding humanism even further. As evolutionists, they change their position as circumstances change. To endeavour to represent humanists fairly, the following clause is quoted from the minimum statement of belief required by the international body: 'Humanism is a democratic and ethical life stance, which affirms that human beings have the right and responsibility to give meaning and shape to their own lives. It stands for the building of a more humane society through an ethic based on human and other natural values in the spirit of reason and free inquiry through human capabilities. It is not theistic, and it does not accept supernatural views of reality.' (IHEU bylaw 5.1)

For our purposes, the key issue is that humanism rejects transcendent revelation in which a higher being (God to Christians) passes down his law. Please note that it clearly states that 'it is not theistic'. It teaches that human beings have evolved to the top of the animal kingdom and are capable of solving all problems by rational thought. Human beings are the final judge of everything. It is optimistic in that it believes that human beings can and will solve all of life's problems. Humanists believe that man is basically good because he possesses 'natural values' with the ability to distinguish between right and wrong. Humanists reject any spiritual dimension in man and do not explain how these 'natural values' evolve. It must be said, however, that many of their values look suspiciously like the Ten Commandments, reminding us of God's words: 'I will put my laws into their minds, and write them on their hearts' (Hebrews 8:10). This is also to be expected as humanism was born during the Enlightenment when the prevailing world view was still Christian. However, humanists also hold some very non-biblical, but politically correct, views on such issues as abortion and gay rights. Humanists believe that all men are equal. Sometimes this is carried to ridiculous lengths, as they believe that anyone can do anything and that everyone is entitled to the same rights and entitlements. Secular humanism and postmodernism (see below) are probably the dominant philosophies shaping our world today.

## Relativism

Relativism is another difficult philosophy to understand because of its many facets. But for our purposes, all that we need to note is that it teaches that there can be no *absolute truth* (except, of course, for this truth!). All truth, including morality and ethics, is relative to our culture, our times and our environment. This is directly at odds with the Christian view that God has revealed *absolute* truth in the Bible and that it applies to all people everywhere and at all times. God does not change and nor does his truth. An extension of relativism is that the *majority* is always 'right', regardless of whether or not this view clashes with the truth that is revealed in the Bible. It gives legitimacy to democracy which the western world tends to idolize.

## Existentialism

Existentialism is a philosophy that probably belongs to past history but aspects of its teaching have permeated much of present-day thinking, including the thinking of people in the church. It has found a ready home in contemporary youth culture. Essentially, existentialism taught that there are no values other than freedom and that human experience is all important. It also stands in direct opposition to objective truth being revealed to us from God. Its lack of values and morals effectively teaches that whatever feels good, is good. Everyone can 'do his own thing'. Have you noticed anyone with this philosophy? Are you free from such thinking?

## Postmodernism

Postmodernism follows modernism in that it places 'I' at the centre of everything. From this, we can conclude that selfishness is good. It incorporates elements of both relativism and existentialism. It teaches that we learn to 'know' through emotions, culture, aesthetics and other 'soft' issues. As a result, knowledge is not founded on objective truths nor on facts. Consequently, we can be certain of nothing. In its extreme form, we can never know any truth, except, of course, this truth about postmodernism. It focuses on relationships, love, shared tradition and integrity *in discussion*. It rejects absolutes and any definition of right versus wrong. This thinking, along with secular humanism, is all pervading in today's secular culture and is at the heart of the view that almost anything should be tolerated, except, perhaps, for evangelical Christianity because of its claim to be exclusively true. It has invaded the church in the so-called 'emerging church movement'. It has also encroached on scientific thinking with scientists (especially biologists in the great environmental debates) arguing that they can 'feel' how the world is changing.

A detailed analysis of postmodernism and its influence on the church is beyond the scope of this book, but interested readers will do well to read D.A. Carson's *Becoming Conversant with the Emerging Church*.[1]

## Behavioural psychology

Behavioural psychology places man at the centre of everything, as does humanism. A key humanist who was voted the American Humanist Association 'humanist of the year' in 1967 was Abraham Maslow. He developed one of the most popular theories of motivation. Other key proponents (and humanists of the year) were B.F. Skinner and Karl Rogers. Another famous theologian-turned-medical scientist and then student of behaviour was the brilliant Russian, Ivan Pavlov. He studied dogs and found that they could be conditioned by external stimuli. Maslow studied monkeys. The key methodology of this branch of psychology is empirical results from experiment or observation. In this methodology, theory is developed by extrapolating from the *specific* to the *general*. In general, this is a flawed philosophical process and has led to criticism of the whole movement. This is especially true when the extrapolation is from animals to human beings! Nevertheless, it is widely accepted in management theory. In fairness, the results may be valid in a particular culture and time if the research is done well. For example, suppose a disinterested scientist studies the behaviour of ten thousand Englishmen between the ages of twenty and forty and concludes that eighty per cent of them like one thing or another. It is reasonable to assume that eighty per cent of all Englishmen of the same age will like the same things. We have extrapolated from the particular (the ten thousand) to the general (all Englishmen), but the conclusion is probably reasonable. It would be wrong to extrapolate this to all Frenchmen and, even worse, to all men. Behaviourism has a place in management and in business when its conclusions are well founded on sound research. It is an attempt to discover the natural laws governing human behaviour and, as such, deserves our attention. It can also predict certain behaviour patterns. Problems arise when conclusions are drawn which contradict the teaching of the Bible or are not based on valid scientific research. As Bible-believing Christians, we can cut the process short by simply studying the behaviour of man in the Bible. After all, God knows all about us and has chosen to reveal a great deal about mankind to us.

Part of the problem with behaviourism is that it seeks to understand and predict human behaviour so that people can be 'conditioned', which, in my view, is a euphemism for *manipulated*. I believe that a great deal of modern management of people is nothing short of manipulation.

We return to Maslow and his hierarchy of human needs. He placed human needs in this order (starting from the bottom):

Self-Actualization
Esteem Needs
Belonging Needs
Safety Needs
Physiological Needs

Maslow believed that man can be motivated by satisfying these needs, moving from the bottom to the top. Frederick Herzberg suggested that environmental factors ('hygiene factors') which were not pleasing to people would lead to *demotivation* and, therefore, had to be removed. Such removal would not lead to motivation but set the stage for positive motivators. Maslow's hierarchy of needs, therefore, went beyond

Herzberg in that he identified needs which, if satisfied, would lead to motivation. Maslow taught that once the bottom four needs have been satisfied, then they no longer work as motivators. Self-actualization is, therefore, the ultimate motivator. I suspect in the real world motivation in business is at root simply feeding greed. As we shall see in chapter 6, much of the motivation on the stock exchange is unfettered greed. In the previous chapter, we considered the ultimate motivator for a Christian to be love (*agape*). But this leaves the manager with a dilemma when managing people who do not profess to be Christians and are, therefore, not driven by the same motivators as we would like to expect. We, therefore, need to take a more detailed look at Maslow to see if something closer to these needs can be found in the Bible or, at least, not be condemned by it. If Maslow's views are not beyond biblical limits, then we may be able to use some of them to some degree. Bear in mind that Maslow was starting from a different point, but because he based his views on what he *observed* about human beings, he was not too far wrong in *some* of his conclusions.

Physiological needs are clearly endorsed in the Bible. Referring to our material needs in general, Jesus said, 'Your heavenly Father knows that you need them all' (Matthew 6:32). No problem with this one. Next, we have safety needs. Throughout the Bible physical safety is simply assumed. Indeed, one of the duties of the king (the state in our times) was the protection of the people. 'Belonging' or social needs come next. Once again the Bible consistently sees people as social creatures. The church consists of those who 'meet together' (Hebrews 10:25). I have consistently argued that we must extrapolate principles that apply in the church to our work. Here is a principle which recognizes that human beings need to belong to one another. So, once again, we endorse Maslow. The last of the four is esteem. To the extent that this means 'respect', there is no problem. Paul argued for mutual respect even in the relationship between master and slave (Ephesians 6:5–9). The manager must show his subordinates respect but let them understand that he is not thereby promoting pride. He must also practise love (*agape*) in his handling of all of his staff. To this point, therefore, our views are not widely divergent from Maslow.

There is, however, concern about 'self-actualization'. It contains too much 'self' (or the 'I' in postmodernism). Basically, it endorses our selfish desire to do what we want instead of what glorifies God. It puts our interest at the centre of what motivates us. Doing work which is satisfying, enjoyable and pays well is a *blessing* from God, but must not be our primary motivation. More important, however, is what Jesus taught. He did not say that self-actualization (or self-fulfilment) should be our desire or right. He said, 'If anyone would come after me, let him *deny* himself and take up his cross daily and follow me' (Luke 9:23, emphasis mine).

We shall now return to the secular view of man. Distilling all of the above, and notwithstanding some acceptance of Maslow, the prevailing *secular* assumptions about people are along these lines:

- People are basically good. All that a manager needs to do is to unlock their inherent goodness. Man can and will solve his problems because man is evolving in every way, including morally, i.e. getting better.
- Human beings have rights (actually entitlements) without the need for any corresponding responsibilities.
- Everyone is equal to everyone else.
- Empirical methods (i.e. studies) are valid in coming to understand human beings, even if these studies are done on animals. No consideration is given to biblical principles.
- It is legitimate to understand, categorize and then manipulate employees.
- Motivation is based on fulfilling a person's needs in a hierarchy, with 'self-actualization' being the ultimate motivator. The underlying assumption is to satisfy selfishness.
- Selfish greed is a human need that can be used to motivate people.
- There are no absolute ethics. In fact, there are no absolutes apart from this one. Everything is relative and we cannot be certain about anything, including what is right or wrong.
- Management focuses on outcomes, sometimes justifying any means if the end is desirable.
- People are entitled to enjoy themselves and should be given the freedom to do what they please.

- There is no requirement to be committed to anything, especially if this curtails a person's freedom or right to do as he pleases.
- Every individual's *feelings* about right and wrong are valid.

By contrast, the Bible says that God knows what is in man because God created man (John 2:25; Psalm 103:14). The biblical view of mankind is, therefore, *realistic* and not optimistic. The natural character of man is revealed to us and is more fully described in the previous chapter. Let us summarize the biblical view as follows:

- People have a dual nature; they are made in God's image and, therefore, possess many unique characteristics but at the same time they are sinful and pursue their own selfish interests.
- We are all equal before God as sinners and in need of the same salvation. We are not all equal in talents, material possessions or opportunity.
- Motivation for the Christian should be based primarily on love (*agape*), first for God and then for others, and on obeying all of God's laws *because we love Him*.
- Rewards for good service and punishment for disobedience are permissible.
- In addition to achieving business outcomes, Christians are called upon to focus on behavioural 'inputs' which are driven by absolute principles, i.e. God's moral law.

The question now arises as to how a Christian executive should treat all of his staff. The answer can be summarized in two principles:

- All people are sinners;
- They must be treated with dignity and respect as image bearers of God.

We shall now expand on these principles and note how each can be applied to the job of the manager.

## Mankind as sinners

As man is a sinner by nature, he can never be fully trusted. This means that we must always build checks and balances around every employee, including ourselves. This is in line with the management principle of 'control' described above.

At every level, man needs to be in what is known as a 'closed loop'. He must account for what he does with the time, money, equipment and people that he manages. The manager must check his subordinate's actions and, then, in turn report to his superiors. Most people resent this hierarchy of 'checking up' but it is essential if one's starting point is that all mankind is basically sinful. If he is set free and allowed to 'self-actualize', he will simply serve his own interests much of the time. In fairness, and recognizing God's universal grace, we acknowledge that countless non-Christian men and women exercise self-control and do act beyond their own interests.

A further consequence of the sinful nature of man is his inability to communicate accurately. The Bible says that the devil has been a liar from the beginning: 'You are of your father the devil, and your will is to do your father's desires. He was a murderer from the beginning, and has nothing to do with the truth, because there is no truth in him. When he lies, he speaks out of his own character, for he is a liar and the father of lies' (John 8:44). Tough words—not mine, but those of Jesus! It takes effort to be absolutely honest and to convey the truth accurately. We must check *ourselves* and be on our guard with what others say.

## Dignity and respect for all

At all times, the Christian manager must remember that all mankind bears God's image. This is true even of the worst person. We must treat everyone with respect and dignity. Does this mean that employees can do what they please and never be disciplined or dismissed? Not at all. The manager must cope with a tension. The balance is between being a good steward of his company's money and treating all subordinates as people made in the image of God. These are not mutually exclusive demands. A good manager will achieve both. (See below for a further discussion on discipline.)

I grew up in apartheid South Africa. One of the less obvious evils of apartheid was the lack of respect given to people of colour, even to the point of black African people losing their own self-respect. Nelson Mandela tells of the first time that he boarded an aeroplane and noticed that the pilot was black. He wanted to get off!

It was the custom in South Africa to refer to black Africans by their first name only. Usually, this was not their real name but a 'western' name that allowed people of European origin to remember and pronounce it. This is also true of Nelson Mandela. A teacher who could not pronounce his real name (Rolihlahla) simply gave him a new one (after Horatio Nelson) which has stuck ever since! On three occasions, I was appointed as the chief executive from outside of the company. One of my early actions in each job was to announce that no apartheid would be practised in any company that I headed up. I was always assured that this was already the policy. To a degree it was true. I then announced that I wanted to meet every single person in the company and that all supervisors were to introduce their subordinates to me, by first and last name (surname). It was amusing to observe white supervisors scurrying around learning to pronounce and remember difficult black African names. Unintentionally, they had failed to treat their black subordinates with the respect due to a person made in God's image. This action on my part was seen as a political statement branding me as a liberal. People were then really confused when I also issued a directive that all 'nude, lewd or rude' posters or calendars had to be removed. What sort of liberal was I? Not one at all. I was just a Christian applying the doctrine of people being made in God's image.

I know a manager who tried hard to get a subordinate to achieve the required standard in her job but to no avail. In the end, the manager decided to dismiss her, which she did with respect for her dignity and real concern for her well-being. The manager worked hard to guide her into a new job and continued to be concerned for her to the extent that ten years later the subordinate joined her former employer on a family holiday. Is this *agape*?

As I said at the beginning of the book, we are given some surprisingly detailed instructions on behaviour at work. Paul, writing to the Ephesians and the Colossians, gave clear instructions to both workers (slaves, in this case) and to managers. Read what he said, 'Slaves, obey your earthly masters with fear and trembling, with a sincere heart, *as you would Christ*, not by the way of eye-service, as people-pleasers, but as servants of Christ, doing the will of God from the heart, rendering service with a good will as to the Lord and not to man, knowing that whatever good anyone does, this he will receive back from the Lord, whether he is a slave or free. Masters, *do the same* to them, and stop your threatening, knowing that he who is both their Master and yours is in heaven, and that there is no partiality with him' (Ephesians 6:5–9, emphasis mine). We have already dealt with the instructions to the slaves. But notice the surprising instructions to the master (read it as manager): 'Do the same to them.' Do what the same? Surely, the phrases that fit this exhortation are 'with a sincere heart', 'as servants of Christ', 'doing the will of God'. Paul's point is summarized in his reminder that both master and slave are under the lordship of Christ. We work for him. In essence, he is saying, 'Be humble.'

## Humility

A Christian manager must be humble at all times. This must not be confused with 'being soft' or 'weak', even though it will be confused by those who do not understand the true meaning of biblical humility. We shall deal with this again under the heading 'leadership', but we need to be reminded here that the opposite of humility is arrogance, not weakness. Being confident that you know what you are doing is good and makes your subordinates feel comfortable, but there is a fine line between *confidence* and *arrogance*. The key is *humility* which is based on Paul's instruction to remember that we are all under the lordship of Christ. Compared to him, we can never be arrogant or boastful. James says, 'God opposes the proud, but gives grace to the humble' (James 4:6).

In chapter 2, I made mention of the black African couple who worked as a messenger and a toilet cleaner respectively. We got to know them well and, despite the huge disparity in our material wealth and the racial difference between us (this was apartheid South Africa), they were completely at ease with us and once spent a very happy holiday in our home. After they left, my wife and I felt that they had contributed more to us (in friendship and humble, godly example) than the little of our material goods that we had shared with them. They understood that they possessed immeasurable riches and shared them willingly. Their focus was on eternal glory. Read these words:

But Jesus called them to him and said, 'You know that the rulers of the Gentiles lord it over them, and their great ones exercise authority over them. It shall not be so among you. But whoever would be great among you must be your servant, and whoever would be first among you must be your slave, even as the Son of Man came not to be served but to serve ...' (Matthew 20:25–28).

I have no doubt that in the kingdom of heaven that black African couple will enjoy highly placed positions. Jesus also said, 'So the last will be first, and the first last' (Matthew 20:16).

In God's economy, there are no celebrities on earth, although I suspect there will be in heaven.

## Discipline

All employees must know what is expected of them and that their manager will hold them accountable for achieving the required outcomes. (Remember my reference to Moses). This is the stewardship role of the manager. All employees should also know that if they fail to do this, they will be disciplined or even dismissed, but with respect and dignity. Justice must be applied, with the employee being given the opportunity to defend himself and, if necessary, to bring in a friend or even a lawyer to help him. We have already shown that all of God's laws, including practising righteousness, must be maintained in all our dealings. If a person has to be disciplined, then divide the actions into two parts: one, *what* must be done and two, *how* to do it. Both must meet biblical standards. There is no room for one-sided ruthlessness.

A Christian manager must be open and honest in assessing his subordinates. Commend them when they do right and correct them when they do wrong. Paul taught that every good parent disciplines his children (Hebrews 12:7) and that 'for the moment all discipline seems painful rather than pleasant, but later it yields the peaceful fruit of righteousness to those who have been trained by it' (Hebrews 12:11). The manager must love (*agape*) his subordinates and treat them with respect and dignity in order to retain their trust and goodwill. Only when a person really accepts that the discipline imposed on him is fair and aimed at *his* improvement, will corrective discipline be received.

## Health and safety

If we truly respect people, every Christian manager will be concerned about the welfare of his staff. I am not referring to bureaucratic risk assessments, reports and other documents which end up in files and make little or no difference to the real safely of the people on the front line. Even worse, this legal work may simply be a means to shift blame, preferably to no one. Naturally, as a Christian, a manager must obey the law and do what it requires, but there is a real danger that he may focus on the *form* of safety rather than on the *substance*, leaving workers at real risk. Worse still, he may simply be absolving himself of any potential blame.

I shall illustrate this by using an example from a refurbishment programme done at the church which I attend. Great pains were taken to do all the things required by the law and all the assessments and plans were created and filed. This is all good. One of the activities was to remove and replace the ceiling. At the same time work continued at ground level. Clearly, everyone on the ground had to wear a hard hat. Then a man was spotted up in the rafters not wearing a hard hat. He argued that for the work he was doing at the time, the hard hat would have been a hindrance and would actually only have added to the risk. In addition, since *he* was above all the work, nothing was likely to fly up to hit him on the head. If he lost his footing and fell to the floor, he would likely fall on his head, but the hard hat might easily get to the ground first and be a hazard on which to fall. Yet the rules required him to wear one. A practical risk assessment might have him wear a *helmet* and maybe a safety harness, but it did not. The rules did not require the wearing of safety boots, despite the fact that the workman believed that this was the only real risk. (Thankfully, they all wore them!) In my view, a Christian manager ensures a person's *real safety*, even if it means doing what no law can ever fully specify. In short, Christian managers cannot hide behind the law and merely observe the regulations but, in reality, still expose subordinates to danger.

Why have we got ourselves into a bureaucratic muddle over safety? I think it is a direct consequence of postmodernism. We no longer believe in absolutes. So, we cannot say to a manager that he has an absolute duty to ensure the real safety of his staff, working out what this may be in any circumstances. Such an instruction relies on biblical concepts of care, concern and love which are not accepted by the secular world. So, all we are left with are the rules, regardless of whether or not they are relevant or make any sense. All a manager has to do to keep out of trouble (maybe his only motivation) is to apply rules in a mechanical fashion. Christians account to a higher authority and must ensure real safety. We do this quite naturally in our families because we *love* them.

## Communication

One of the greatest problems in any organization (not limited to companies) is communication. As human beings, we find it difficult to communicate accurately even if our intention is to be honest. We are often misunderstood or taken out of context. These situations will occur but we should strive to avoid *causing* them. Even Jesus was misquoted (John 21:22–23). Every manager should set the example in this regard. He should endeavour to communicate transparently with his staff, telling them as much as he can and trying to be as open as he can be. He may never tell any sort of untruth—there is no such thing as a white lie, only a lie.

We have already dealt with the communication that calls for our yes to be 'yes' and our no to be 'no' (James 5:12). Regrettably, in Anglo Saxon culture the word 'yes' can mean anything from 'affirmative' to 'negative' and every possible meaning in between depending on the emphasis, context or body language. Perhaps, this is just part of our language, but it can give rise to misunderstanding and even mistrust. Why not just use the words with their conventional meaning?

I am a positive person. I tend to see 'the glass half full' and, therefore, tend to 'round up'. It is a danger to do so and I am grateful for faithful subordinates who have issued a word of caution if they thought that I had painted too rosy a picture. The same can be argued in reverse for those who are of a negative disposition. The key issue is always to try to paint an *accurate* picture. Those in media work have the hardest job with respect to this. It is difficult to report on a situation without bias, but accuracy is a discipline that needs constant practice by all of us.

We must learn to say the same thing directly to a person that we would say about that person to others. Otherwise, we are 'bearing false witness' and breaking the ninth commandment. I am always amazed at how easily we slip into conveying entirely different messages to different audiences. This should not be so.

The medium of communication is also important. Human beings want social interaction. This is at the heart of being called upon to meet together as a church (Hebrews 10:25). Few of us have the literary skills to communicate in writing and this should never be a substitute for face to face communication. The great privilege which Moses enjoyed was that 'the LORD used to speak to Moses face to face, as a man speaks to his friend' (Exodus 33:11). The Romans only permitted an accuser to meet the accused 'face to face' (Acts 25:16). John had this to say, 'Though I have much to write to you, I would rather not use paper and ink. Instead I hope to come to you and talk face to face, so that our joy may be complete' (2 John 12). In his great chapter on love, Paul said, 'We see in a mirror dimly, but then face to face' (1 Corinthians 13:12). We should also note the example of Paul when he disagreed with Peter. He said, 'I opposed him to his face, because he stood condemned' (Galatians 2:11). Paul was prepared to confront the great apostle Peter 'to his face' after he had just referred to him as a 'pillar' (v. 9).

When I was running companies, I banned internal memos unless they simply recorded such information as facts, specifications and the like. An analysis of any company's internal communications will reveal that it is seldom used to keep others informed (which is what it is supposed to do) but is used for political ends. We are now blessed with improved communications in that we can use e-mails, telephones, video conferencing and webcams very cheaply. All this is a help, but the best method is face to face. During my period in office, I encouraged this and never objected to heavy travel bills if it was in the interests of improved communication.

Now we have e-mail! In many ways it is a blessing, but we are right back to written communications and a *greatly improved means of playing office politics*. I would have liked to ban it for internal communication but I guess it is too late for that now. So, be careful how you communicate with your fellow workers by e-mail. Reread all e-mails, checking for any ambiguities or any insulting comments whether intended or not. Avoid any sensitive issues which are best dealt with by face to face meetings. Do not deal with anything negative by e-mail.

## Division of work

Work is clearly divided into various disciplines and allocated according to a person's skills. Fine examples occur in the building and operation of the tabernacle and, then again, in Solomon's Temple: 'So now send me a man skilled to work in gold, silver, bronze, and iron, and in purple, crimson, and blue fabrics, trained also in engraving, to be with the skilled workers who are with me in Judah and Jerusalem' (2 Chronicles 2:7).

The New Testament also sets out the principles for the identifying and utilizing of people's gifts (1 Corinthians 12; Romans 12:6–8). The context is the church, but we affirmed at the beginning of this book that general biblical principles can, and should, be applied to our work environment. These passages teach us what we probably know from nature, namely, that no two human beings are alike and none of us can do everything. It is one of Adam Smith's principles. A key task of every executive is, therefore, to discover the gifts of each subordinate and to endeavour to develop these gifts and use them to the mutual advantage of the individual and the company. This is what Solomon did so well. Each person should also be encouraged to discover his own gifts. Read what the apostle Paul had to say, 'I say to everyone among you not to think of himself more highly than he ought to think, but to think with sober judgement' (Romans 12:3). He continues, 'Having gifts that differ according to the grace given to us, let us use them…' (Romans 12:6). When employees really examine themselves and also trust the judgement of their manager with respect to what they can do, there will be 'round pegs in round holes' and 'square pegs in square holes'. If this does not happen, there will be untold misery.

## Honesty and integrity

As a manager, one needs to set the example of honesty and integrity. We dealt with this in the previous chapter as well as in the paragraph dealing with communications. The manager has the special task of ensuring that everyone falls into line. Teach and encourage staff to tell the truth at all times. This is especially true with respect to customers. If a delivery is going to be late, have the appropriate person call the customer and tell him. It may be appropriate to give reasons but, sometimes, this may appear to be transferring blame and, at other times, it may be embarrassing unnecessarily someone who is made in God's image. I recently heard a valuable quip: 'Always tell the truth but don't always be telling.'

I can recall an occasion when something had gone badly wrong in a department. I called the manager concerned and asked him to find out and let me now how this had gone wrong. His answer was amazingly frank: 'I can tell you right now,' he said, 'I messed this up all by myself.' Could I help laughing? His honesty got me on his side and we worked together to rectify the situation. On another occasion, a serious breach of discipline was reported to me on the part of one of the senior members of the executive team. He was a very competent person and this breach would possibly lead to his dismissal. I was very disappointed. Before I could even send for him, he asked to see me. As soon as he sat down, he said something along these lines: 'I have come to tell you what I did. I am ashamed of myself and I feel I let you and the company down.' He proceeded to give me an accurate account of what had happened. At all the subsequent hearings, no one ever gave a more accurate account of what happened than he did. He then offered his resignation, which I could not accept because one cannot avoid discipline by resigning. The point of this anecdote is that I was dealing with a man of absolute integrity who had succumbed in a moment of temptation. (At that stage, he was not a Christian but I am pleased to say that before long he was, and he is now in glory.)

## Motivation

We dealt with motivation in the previous chapter. In practice, the manager must motivate his staff. As has been stated, many of these will not hold his Christian views and, therefore, will not be motivated by the *agape* love that should motivate staff who are Christians. So, how does the Christian manager motivate all of his staff?

We return to Maslow and the other behaviourists. I can find no fault with the basic idea that people will be motivated by satisfying legitimate needs. These are (in ascending order) physical, social, safety, esteem and self-actualization. I have expressed reservations about the last need insofar as Christians are concerned, because a Christian should respond to a higher command—that is, 'to love' (*agape*). However, I suspect that in most businesses it is much more straightforward than that. The underlying method of motivation is simply to appeal to people's greed. How do we handle this?

Clearly, we cannot judge other people's motives nor can we be held responsible for their actions. Nevertheless, we should strive not to be the *cause* of leading people into sin. Jesus said, 'Woe to the world for temptations to sin! For it is necessary that temptations come, but woe to the one by whom the temptation comes!' (Matthew 18:7). I repeat, we must avoid leading people into sin. Consequently, commission or bonus schemes should make it clear that such payments are meant as a reward for work well done or as a means of sharing in the success of the enterprise and not to satisfy greed. Christian staff members should be given warnings about greed. Oddly, in my career the person who was most against greed did not profess to be a Christian. It is one of those cases where we see God's universal grace at work, writing his law in their hearts (Romans 2:15).

## Remuneration

How much should people be paid?

The matter of pay occurs in the Bible by reminding us that 'the labourer deserves his wages' (1 Timothy 5:18). It also condemns those who *rob* workers of their rightful wages (James 5:4) and warns 'against those who oppress the hired worker in his wages' (Malachi 3:5). This can be by *withholding* pay from them or by *underpaying* them. We must be careful not to do either.

In the parable of the labourers, Jesus departed from the concept of treating everyone 'fairly'—as the humanists would have us do—in the matter of wages. While this parable is not primarily about wages—its meaning is intended to be spiritual—it is inconceivable that Jesus would have used an example which itself was not true. I quote the entire parable:

For the kingdom of heaven is like a master of a house who went out early in the morning to hire labourers for his vineyard. After agreeing with the labourers for a denarius a day, he sent them into his vineyard. And going out about the third hour he saw others standing idle in the marketplace, and to them he said, 'You go into the vineyard too, and whatever is right I will give you.' So they went. Going out again about the sixth hour and the ninth hour, he did the same. And about the eleventh hour he went out and found others standing. And he said to them, 'Why do you stand here idle all day?' They said to him, 'Because no one has hired us.' He said to them, 'You go into the vineyard too.' And when evening came, the owner of the vineyard said to his foreman, 'Call the labourers and pay them their wages, beginning with the last, up to the first.' And when those hired about the eleventh hour came, each of them received a denarius. Now when those hired first came, they thought they would receive more, but each of them also received a denarius. And on receiving it they grumbled at the master of the house, saying, 'These last worked only one hour, and you have made them equal to us who have borne the burden of the day and the scorching heat.' But he replied to one of them, 'Friend, I am doing you no wrong. Did you not agree with me for a denarius? Take what belongs to you and go. I choose to give to this last worker as I give to you. Am I not allowed to do what I choose with what belongs to me? Or do you begrudge my generosity?' (Matthew 20:1–15).

What do we learn from this parable apart from its true spiritual meaning? Firstly, being generous is the master's right. It is actually the duty of the rich. Furthermore, we do not have to engage in 'being fair' with respect to *relative* earnings. There was no extra compensation for the work done for twelve hours compared to one hour. So much of the effort in modern salary and wage schemes arises from the idea that we should either pay everyone the same amount or that any differential must be based on some objective difference (a humanistic principle). If the objective difference is not 'hours worked', then it must be 'grade' or some other contrived explanation. An entire industry of consultants has grown up whose task it is to establish 'grades', evaluate jobs and set the 'correct' salary or wage for every job. Jesus taught that this is not necessary and, indeed, it clashes directly with the concept of the market determining the value of everything, including that of labour. So, how do we know how much to pay a person? Do we get the salary or wage *from the market*? What is 'the market'? When a business finds the right person for a position, it finds out how much it will have to pay him to lure him into the company. That *is* the market, provided that the net has been thrown wide enough to take a sample of the market salaries. Most companies also have employees who leave. It is important to find out why. If it is because they can earn more in the *same* sort of job (not a promotion), then *that* is the market. If people simply grumble but stay in their jobs, then they are at least being paid the market rate. All attempts to 'grade' jobs in order to justify a rate for the job are a waste of time and based on pseudo-science at best. Let me illustrate this point from the National Health Service in Great Britain. According to the British newspaper the *Daily Telegraph* of 10 January 2007, questions were asked in Parliament about the 'very large pay increases' given to medical consultants (specialists) and doctors. It presumably followed some grading exercise by a management consultant. Yet, according to the questioner, each post advertised for a doctor received an average of 210 applicants, indicating a serious *over supply* which should have resulted in the salaries *falling*. (The law of supply and demand.) On 21 April 2007, the National Health Service confirmed this by reporting that there were *ten thousand* surplus doctors and, therefore, young doctors would be encouraged to do voluntary work abroad. However, everyone living in Britain knows that there must be a serious *shortage* because there are long waiting lists to see almost every kind of consultant and perform every kind of procedure. Clearly, therefore, there are too *few posts*. Who decides how many posts there should be? On what basis? The only possible answer is that planners, trying to meet budgets, have kept the number of posts too low, despite the fact that there is an oversupply of personnel but, at the same time, a critical shortage of doctors working in the Health Service. The problem is that a government monopoly does not allow market forces to sort out both the resource problem and the salary of each doctor. If free market forces determined all of these issues, there would be *more* doctors working in the Health Service but each would receive a *lower* salary and patients would receive better service—which is what every business should be striving for. To be fair to the British Health Service, this sort of problem also exists in countries who claim to have a free market in health care. But do they really? Have the professional bodies not raised the barriers to entry in order to create *artificial* shortages so as to raise salaries? *Any tampering* with the market by governments, professional bodies or anyone else will stop the optimizing of resources with supply and demand.

Finally, there is the matter of rewards. In the parable of the faithful stewards (Matthew 25:14–30), the servants who performed well were commended and *promoted*. Notice the commendation: 'Well done, good and faithful servant,' followed by the reward, 'I will set you over much. Enter into the joy of your master.'

Sound management practice recognizes good achievement. But notice what happened to the non-performing servant. His master did not say, 'Too bad, you had better draw welfare.' No, he was punished for not obeying his master and not doing anything with his talent. In fact, he was *severely* punished ('cast ... into the outer darkness'). We live in a culture in which punishment is frowned upon—not so in the Bible. Failure to obey is always followed by discipline. Consequently, there is everything right in recognizing and rewarding good achievements but also disciplining non-performance if it is caused by disobedience or some other moral failure. (Failure to achieve when attempting in good faith to do so is not a sin and should not be punished. It may call for training or simply encouraging.) This approach to rewards and punishment is known as the 'carrot and stick' method of motivation. It is not politically correct!

There is a world of difference between receiving a reward for a job well done and sheer unfettered and selfish greed. The basic difference lies in one's attitude. Greed is born of covetousness and soon overcomes anyone who does not deal with it. Only God can deliver us but we can employ the antidote, namely, to *give* generously if we do receive large rewards. If we fail to deal with greed, we shall soon be breaking the first commandment by idolizing money and making it a god.

## Justice and fairness

In all his dealings, the manager should seek to be just and fair in terms of the principles established in the Bible. 'Masters, treat your slaves *justly and fairly*, knowing that you also have a Master in heaven' (Colossians 4:1, emphasis mine). This may not be the same concept of fairness as that taught by humanistic thinking which is dedicated to 'equality' and 'rights'. We have already seen one example of inequality when Jesus pointed out that a person working one hour could be paid the same as one working for twelve hours. This is unacceptable to the humanist who believes that all men are equal and must receive the same of everything—even to the point of sharing misery equally. This is the underlying reason why secular politicians ensure that education, health care, welfare and other such services will be reduced to the lowest level to ensure that no one gets any more than anyone else. There will be differences in what people contribute and they may be rewarded differently.

Fairness carries with it the concept of justice. Rules of justice are set out in the Bible and include such protective measures as two witnesses for every accusation and punishment which is commensurate with the infringement. Consequently, in our dealings with staff, we should presume innocence, hear the other side of every story and make sure that an employee is given every opportunity to defend himself. In every promotion or reward, we must endeavour to be fair in considering everyone.

## Stewardship

We dealt with stewardship in the previous chapter with respect to the protection of the employer's (or shareholder's) interests. But a manager is to be a good steward of all that is entrusted to him. This includes the people under his management. This is only possible if he really loves (*agape*) them and seeks their best interest and not his own. This cannot simply be at the *expense* of his employer's interest which will always have to be balanced with the individual's interest. Being a manager implies that a person will have the wisdom to achieve this balance. He will encourage and train his subordinates to be more effective in their jobs, making them more useful to the organization, as well as improving themselves.

## Summary of chapter 3

Management theories derived from behaviourism are acceptable insofar as they are based on sound observation of human behaviour and are, at worst, not contradicted by the Bible. But Christians do differ in their assumptions about human beings and add much more that is commanded in the Bible. The Christian manager seeks to glorify God through his example and behaviour, especially in humble, servant leadership.

We are to manage or relate to other people, noting their dual nature which means:

- That people are not basically good but sin touches every faculty;
- That we are, nevertheless, to show everyone respect and dignity because they are made in God's image.

The basic rule for promoting people is based on 'faithful in little, ruler of much'.

Subordinates should be disciplined for disobedience or moral failure and rewarded for outstanding work.

All temptation to greed must be avoided.

## Case studies

### CASE STUDY 1

What if the lowest wage, whatever that is, is not a 'living wage'? We have seen that Malachi is saying that it is possible to *oppress* workers by the wages being paid to them. We also recall that the Christian never pushes his advantage of power to the limit. (This is the principle of fair exchange.) So, clearly, there is some lower limit. In many countries, including both the UK and USA, there is a statutory minimum wage. This, at least, answers the question for managers in those countries, although I would take issue with the concept of this in nations that have people out of work. But what if there is no minimum wage or if this minimum is inadequate? I shall endeavour to answer that from an example from my own experience.

We won a large order in Malaysia in the early 1990s. It received considerable publicity and I found myself being attacked by 'politically correct' people because I was doing business in a corrupt and inhumane country. (So they said. They had the same opinion of the USA.) Shortly afterwards, I had occasion to have a meal with a senior politician from the ruling party in Malaysia. I put my problem to him. He answered along these lines:

In their opinion, the task of every government was to provide opportunity for all people to enjoy security: health care, education, housing, food and work. Malaysia had not accepted aid from anyone. They wanted everyone to work and by the 1990s they had achieved full employment and an impressive record in all the other areas listed above. This was accomplished by ensuring a free market, by *not* introducing a minimum wage and not keeping people out of work by putting them on generous welfare packages. Everyone, therefore, had the opportunity to get employment, even if the starting wage was very low because he could work his way up rather than be 'entitled' to a higher starting wage. This is known as the 'upwardly mobile' labour market. We experienced this in our Malaysian company. Every time we needed to fill a post, we were amazed at the zeal with which employees at lower levels applied for every higher ranked job. No one, it seemed, stayed long at the lowest wage. It was part of Malaysian culture to start at the bottom and work one's way up. This also motivated employees to work hard. My best friend (and major customer) in Malaysia was a very well educated, refined person. He told me that he still lived near his parents who were peasants and who could neither read nor write. In one generation, Malaysia had moved from what was once regarded as a 'basket case' to a thriving modern industrial country. I am not holding Malaysia up as a general example. I simply want to illustrate that there is no simple way to determine when a wage is too low. By allowing the market to find its own level, everyone benefits. In a free labour market, each employer must determine what he can afford to pay the lowest paid workers but, at the same time, not put himself in a position where he can be accused (by God) of 'oppressing' the workers. Clearly, it will differ significantly from society to society.

**CASE STUDY 2**

In the early 1990s, I was fascinated by the Japanese. They seemed to have found a different model by which to do business and somehow two plus two equalled more than four! I wanted to find out the secret. Shortly, thereafter, we found an opportunity to set up a joint venture with a giant Japanese trading house. We would own 40 per cent of the business and they would own 60 per cent. We would nominate the chairman and they would nominate the managing director. By and large, we would supply all other staff and do the accounts. At the end of the first year, we had made a profit to everyone's surprise. The Japanese managing director then asked to see our financial director and we thought that he was merely wishing to discuss the accounts. However, he had a very different mission which taught us a lesson we had not expected to learn. He asked if we were happy with our share of the profits. Of course, we were. They were 40 per cent of the total which was in line with our share of the company. 'No,' explained the managing director, 'that is not what I am asking. Are you really *happy*? Or do you want more?' We were mystified. He was surprised at our surprise, so he went on to explain. In a joint venture, each party must look *after the other party's interest*, not his own. Self-interest is not the Japanese way. 'It is like a good marriage,' he went on to say. 'If the husband looks after his interest and the wife hers, the marriage fails. If the husband sets out to make his wife happy and the wife tries to make her husband happy, then the marriage will be a success. It is the same in business.' I did learn something about Japanese business but it was not what I had expected. I should have known this already because it is none other than (*agape*) love. Incidentally, I also discovered that in Japan two plus two does make four!

**CASE STUDY 3**
Soon after joining Plessey S.A. as managing director, I attended a talk by the head of personnel for the British factory of a Japanese car manufacturer. He explained that they had eliminated clock cards for factory workers. Every day on arrival or departure, employees would insert their cards into a machine which would then record the hours spent at the factory. This information was then used to calculate the weekly wages of the employees. On hearing this, it immediately struck me that clock cards reduced human beings to some sort of machine and did not

recognize that they possessed the dignity of creatures made in God's image. I persuaded others (with little resistance) to abolish the practice in our factories and not only replace it with something more human, but change the entire way that we managed our factory staff, learning what we could from the British factory.

We divided the factory into small groups called 'cells', each working in a partitioned-off area of the factory. They were fully responsible for their area, including its décor and cleanliness. Each cell had a leader who was responsible for setting daily targets for his or her team and then encouraging them to achieve continuously higher outputs. This leader also had to welcome every member of his or her team each shift, usually having them sign in each morning. They did not, however, have to give the time of arrival. It was up to the leader to ensure punctuality and to keep everyone in his or her cell working a full day. If anyone did not come to work at all, then the leader had to find out why. This was not so much to 'check up' on them (they were entitled to be sick for three days without a doctor's certificate), but to find out if all was well. This often unearthed other 'human' problems which led to other programmes to assist our employees.

The outcome was both interesting and highly rewarding. Factory output increased, absenteeism declined and morale improved. But the most surprising result was in time keeping. After a few days, some leaders complained that a substantial group of employees consistently arrived late for work. Upon investigation, it was found that at least one bus was never scheduled to arrive at the factory on time. All employees on this bus had been late for as long as anyone could remember! But all clock cards had always shown their arrival as being on time. Upon further investigation, we discovered that friends had simply loaded the cards of the late employees. If you treat people like machines, they will respond in a machinelike manner! We had the bus company change its schedule and all was well thereafter. Treating people as image bearers of God is correct in every way.

## Discussion questions

1. How does a manager get staff to accomplish the required results if his

staff are weakly committed, demotivated and hold a secular world view?

2. Discuss ways in which integrity could be improved in your work situation.

3. How does your ethnic or cultural background affect your communications?

4. Draw up a table comprising three columns. In the first, describe a typical colleague at work. In the second, describe a typical Christian colleague, if you have any. In the third, describe the characteristics of what a Christian colleague at work should be. Here is a hint: use the characteristics discussed in this chapter.

# Leadership

The greatest leader the world has ever known is Jesus Christ. Consider the facts. He lived two thousand years ago as an extremely poor man in an insignificant country. He appointed twelve men with little to commend them to carry on his work after he died. One failed completely. Then he died an ignominious death on a cross, and with only a handful of his friends and family members present. Maybe a few thousand, or even just a few hundred, followers had been convinced by his message during his short two to three years of teaching. Most had misunderstood him. His followers were devastated by his death as none of their hopes had been fulfilled. Yet two thousand years later, approximately one-third of all people living claim him to be their leader! (I am not suggesting that one-third of the world is truly Christian.) So, we shall be examining his leadership in more detail to see if, by emulating his style, we can become better leaders.

Firstly, we must define what we mean by the term 'leadership'. I suggest a very simple definition: 'to lead' means 'to gain a following'. In some of our minds, the word conjures up a picture of some charismatic and, perhaps, domineering figure who naturally attracts a following because of his *personality, competence or some other visible quality*. He can speak persuasively and gets others to do what he asks. He inspires and motivates people to achieve even what they might otherwise not have done. But, under the surface, there will often be a brutal ruthlessness and a big ego. Some of these points may be valid, but is this the description of a biblical leader? Surely, Hitler was such a figure, and history is not short of others who obtained followers but whom we do not want to hold up as examples. The second question to be answered is: 'What are those following the leader to achieve?' In business, it is usually to achieve the objectives of the unit being led. That is fair enough but that is not what Jesus did. He led people to become disciples—that is, to do what he *did* and be *like him*. This is the ultimate leadership: trying to *inspire* one's subordinates to imitate one's best qualities and to do what the leader does. This, of course, puts pressure on leaders to develop leadership characteristics and to do the right things.

In the previous chapter, we saw that leadership is a component of management. However, leadership as found in management is not the full definition. Some managers are good at implementing plans but are not great leaders in the sense that they inspire others and get a following. Some leaders are not great managers because they are weak when it comes to the details of management that have already been looked at. We are dealing here with broader and more subtle attributes that are part of a person's *character* rather than his *personality*, although the two are often confused. We shall, therefore, look more closely at what makes an exemplary character.

A good leader will not attract people to *himself* for his own selfish ends or to boost his ego. He will *focus* his followers on wider issues than himself. Jesus *did* attract people to himself, but he did so in order that they might become disciples and glorify his Father: 'For I have come down from heaven, not to do my own will but the will of him who sent me' (John 6:38).

So, every good leader does what best *serves* his patients, his students, his team, his shareholders, his company or his organization. It also means leading in the best interests of one's customers, patients, students, subordinates and even one's suppliers. Leadership is not about feeding an ego, or boasting, or flaunting power. It is always focused on the cause of the organization that is being served.

Jesus certainly created a following which is what he intended. Matthew records the words 'follow me' at least six times. The other Gospels also make mention of this invitation often and the entire narrative of Jesus' life leaves one with the impression that everywhere Jesus went he attracted a following of both men and women. It is worth noting that this balance between the genders is not being achieved today because we are presenting an inadequate picture of Jesus which does not always appeal to men. As we go through Jesus' leadership qualities, we shall gain a more balanced view of him.

People followed Jesus when he was on earth and have continued to do so ever since. Why?

## Authority

Jesus attracted a following on account of the authority he demonstrated: '… and they were astonished at his teaching, for his word possessed authority' (Luke 4:32). What is authority? How is it sensed? Jesus had authority because people recognized the truth of what he had to say and the fact that he would accomplish what he said. He demonstrated this again and again: 'And they were all amazed, so that they questioned among themselves, saying, "What is this? A new teaching *with authority*! He *commands* even the unclean spirits, and *they obey* him"'(Mark 1:27, emphasis mine). We also notice that the steward who was entrusted with a small task and succeeded was rewarded with more *authority*. 'And he said to him, "Well done, good servant! Because you have been faithful in a very little, you shall have *authority* over ten cities"' (Luke 19:17, emphasis mine). A good leader builds up his authority by consistently *doing what he says he will do*. Idle boasting has the opposite effect. Superficially, Jesus attracted a following because he healed people. But this is only an explanation in part. Had he sometimes failed, his following would have diminished. The key is that the crowds knew that *he did what he said he would do*.

## Vision

Jesus had vision. Vision is seeing what will happen in the future and being confident about how to shape the future to exploit it or, at least, cope with it. Most people are fearful of the future and, therefore, will follow someone who approaches it with confidence. Jesus knew exactly what would happen, and many examples of him teaching his disciples about the future are recorded in the Gospels. Read Matthew chapters 24–26 or John chapter 14 as examples. Obviously, no one can know the future as Jesus did, but a key element, possibly *the* key element of leadership, is vision. People will follow someone to the extent that they are convinced that that person will lead them into the future and accomplish what it is that he (and they) are seeking to do. To be effective, one needs to think about and work out how to exploit new opportunities, create a future, minimize threats or offer security. Then this needs to be communicated clearly, unambiguously and confidently to those who are to follow. This is 'vision' in action which is also referred to as 'strategy'. No true strategic planning is possible unless it commences with a 'dream' or 'vision'. (See Paul as an example under the heading 'Paul's leadership' later in this chapter.)

## Purpose

When Jesus stood before Pilate, he resolutely faced the cross because he knew what he had come to do: 'Then Pilate said to him, "So you are a king?" Jesus answered, "You say that I am a king. For this purpose I was born and for this purpose I have come into the world—to bear witness to the truth"' (John 18:37). Jesus knew what he aimed to achieve and never swerved from that goal. No fewer than eight times in the Gospel of Luke alone, does he use the words 'had to' or 'must'. For a leader to secure a following, he must know what his purpose is and be able to communicate that to his subordinates. Please note the great strength in Jesus' resoluteness—nothing soft or weak about him!

## Servant leadership

One of the most remarkable attributes of Jesus' leadership was his willingness to be a servant. This is not what came to mind when we conjured up a mental picture of a personality leader. Can you imagine Hitler behaving like a servant? Note the contrast between our concept of a leader and Jesus: 'When *he had washed their feet* and put on his outer garments and resumed his place, he said to them, "Do you understand what I have done to you? You call me Teacher and Lord, and you are right, for so I am. If I then, your Lord and Teacher, have washed your feet, you also ought to wash one another's feet. For I have given you an example, that *you also should do just as I have done to you*"' (John 13:12–15, emphasis mine). To understand fully what Jesus had done, we must remember that the lowest rank of slaves washed the feet of guests. It was not a pleasant job in a hot, dry and dusty country. Please note also the reason why he did it. Washing feet was not his normal job and he was not suggesting that he should exchange his usual job for washing feet. What he did was to serve as 'an example'. He was demonstrating an attitude. Servant leadership is not giving up your leadership role by becoming a servant. It is *leading* with the *intent* to serve others. It is having the correct attitude.

The application of this servant leadership role in a modern workplace needs deliberate practical application. A good leader will not doubt his role and hence not mind doing anything, however lowly. He must be prepared to help his subordinates, even doing the most menial of tasks. After all, Jesus found time to wash his disciples feet! Clearly, this may introduce a conflict. On the one hand, the leader will be earning a higher salary than his subordinates and will, in all probability, be pressed for time. Am I suggesting that the leader wastes his precious time doing menial tasks that could be done by people who are paid lower wages? No, a leader must be a good steward of his time and not waste his (expensive) time. But there will be occasions when everyone will be together and only one person can perform a menial task. Then, the leader should be the first to volunteer to do the lowest job. Here is a simple example. The staff are all in a conference and drinks are to be served. Everyone stops working. Who will act as the server? The leader will. Another example is in the preparation of a proposal or a report. The leader may be present to offer advice and may be waiting to sign the document. He then offers to do the photocopying as well. This is servant leadership. A leader should never cut himself off in the proverbial 'ivory tower'.

## As a shepherd

One of the pictures of leadership which occurs several times in the New Testament is that of a shepherd. Jesus said of himself, 'I am the good shepherd. The good shepherd lays down his life for the sheep' (John 10:11). He goes on to say, 'I know my own and my own know me' (John 10:14). The expression 'to know a person' rather than 'to know something *about* a person' is always a description of a relationship. In this context, where Jesus explains that 'the good shepherd lays down his life for the sheep', he is, in fact, saying the same thing as 'Greater love has no one than this, that someone lays down his life for his friends' (John 15:13). He is saying that a good shepherd *loves (agape)* his sheep to the point of giving his life for them. This is a tough lesson for us to learn. A good leader must *love (agape)* his subordinates. This means he must act in *their best interest* and not his own. He must care about them, respect them, help them, go out of the way for them.

I shall illustrate real concern for a subordinate by using the example of a president of one of our companies. He was abroad but had to cut short his trip due to the sudden death of a subordinate. On the Saturday afternoon, he had the emotional task of speaking at the funeral. That night, emotionally drained, seriously jetlagged and tired, he went to bed early. During this time, another subordinate's newly born baby died and he and his wife were in need of comfort and support. Who did they call? The president of the company who got up and spent the remainder of the night with them. Surely, this is good stewardship of people motivated by (*agape*) love.

This principle applies even if there is little liking for the people concerned. Read what Jesus had to say on the subject: 'You have heard that it was said, "You shall love your neighbour and hate your enemy." But I say to you, Love your enemies and pray for those who persecute you' (Matthew 5:43–44).

Jesus uses the imagery of being a shepherd again and again. It occurs no fewer than eleven times in the Gospels. It is, therefore, not surprising that we find the apostle Peter taking up the theme as he gives instructions to the elders. However, I must add a word of warning. All too often the image that has been added by sentimentalists is one of a *soft* Jesus carrying little lambs in his arms. This is not how Jesus described himself. He was a courageous and brave shepherd, the kind that lay at the door of the fold and fought off the wild beast to the point of sacrificing his own life for his sheep.

## Paul's leadership

There are many excellent leaders mentioned in the Bible and we could fruitfully study them all because there is no one 'type'. I shall, however, focus my attention on Paul because he suggested that we 'join in imitating [him], and keep [our] eyes on those who walk according to the example [we] have in [him]' (Philippians 3:17). He was not asking us to imitate him as a person but as a follower of Christ. He had just said, 'Not that I have already obtained this or am already perfect, but I press on to make it my own, *because Christ Jesus has made me his own*. Brothers, I do not consider that I have made it my own' (Philippians 3:12–13, emphasis mine).

Paul secured a following even when he was officially at the bottom of the ladder. Consider the shipwreck incident of Acts chapter 27. At first the centurion and the ship's pilot did not listen to Paul but after a while they not only listened, but also did precisely as he advised. He was a prisoner! His leadership was with authority and it produced a following.

Paul was gentle even when he had to be tough. Notice how he dealt with a difficult Corinthian church: 'For this reason I write these things while I am away from you, that when I come I may not have to be severe in my use of the authority that the Lord has given me for building up and not for tearing down' (2 Corinthians 13:10). As leaders, we are called upon to exercise authority, but in a way which seeks to 'build up' and is sensitive to the feelings of the recipients.

Paul commended several people for working hard (Romans 16; Colossians 4) but he set the example: 'I worked harder than any of them, though it was not I, but the grace of God that is with me' (1 Corinthians 15:10). A leader should never misuse his position by letting others do the work. He should always be at the front, doing the hardest work.

Paul believed in encouraging others and constantly commended many 'little people'. Read Brian Edwards' book *Little people in Paul's letters*[1] for more of these. Here are just few: Epaphras, Epaphroditus, Tychicus, Onesimus, John Mark, Aquila and Priscilla. Paul must have realized that expressing appreciation in a letter (a big event in those days) would be a great reward for these 'little' people. A good leader tries to find something to appreciate in all of his followers. Expressing public appreciation in the right way is the mark of a good leader.

Paul also followed Jesus in ensuring succession. Jesus chose twelve disciples to carry on after he left this world. One failed, but the rest as well as men like Paul, Luke and James had been trained to continue the work. Today, as we said at the start of this chapter, one-third of the world claims to have Jesus as their leader. Paul, likewise, had developed men like Timothy and Titus. It behoves all leaders to train those who will carry on after they leave office. Some will fail (as Judas did) and others will fail initially as both Peter and Mark did. But Paul never gave up on Mark. He later wrote, 'Luke alone is with me. Get Mark and bring him with you, for he is very useful to me for ministry' (2 Timothy 4:11).

Paul had a *vision* to preach the gospel to the Gentiles throughout the then-known world. He translated this into a plan and a strategy. Note the details he outlines to the Romans: 'But now, since I no longer have any room for work in these regions, and since I have longed for many years to come to you, I hope to see you in passing as I go to Spain, and to be helped on my journey there by you, once I have enjoyed your company for a while. At present, however, I am going to Jerusalem bringing aid to the saints' (Romans 15:23–25). 'When therefore I have completed this and have delivered to them what has been collected, I will leave for Spain by way of you' (Romans 15:28). These plans did not come about quite as Paul had hoped because God had other plans for him, but Paul did not know the details of God's plans and *so planned as best he could at the time*. We should always plan in accordance with our vision but, as James points out, add the words 'God willing'.

Paul was courageous. He wrote of the many trials that befell him: shipwrecks, beatings and imprisonment. A leader will catch all of the criticism and may not get any recognition or reward in this life. Paul described his life as a 'fight' but one which promised a crown in heaven (2 Timothy 4:6–8). All leaders need to do this in whatever job they find themselves, always with an eye on eternal rewards (Colossians 3:24).

Finally, Paul believed in teamwork and a study of his life reveals that he always chose to be with 'fellow workers'. One of the saddest verses penned by Paul was when he wrote with understandable hyperbole '... all deserted me. May it not be charged against them!' (2 Timothy 4:16). A study of Ephesians 2:5–6 reveals that eleven times in the passage the prefix *sun* is used in the description of what Christ has done for us. This prefix means 'together'. It does not come out in every instance in modern translations of the Bible. Paul said 'made alive *together*', 'raised us up *together*', 'seated *together*' and so forth. Every leader should strive to lead a *team* that works *together*. This is never easy, but true leadership endeavours to get the most out of people and this will always be more effective if everyone is pulling together.

## Example from the elders

The passage quoted next is aimed at the elders and the church. So, we may question how this applies to a leader in a work environment. Remember that we are trying to find examples of good *leadership* which we can imitate in our work. Absolute principles of leadership are being taught which we can apply to any situation. Therefore, we shall look carefully at 1 Peter 5:1–6.

So I exhort the elders among you ... shepherd the flock of God that is among you, exercising oversight, not under compulsion, but willingly, as God would have you; not for shameful gain, but eagerly; not domineering over those in your charge, but being examples to the flock. And when the chief Shepherd appears, you will receive the unfading crown of glory ... Clothe yourselves, all of you, with humility towards one another, for God opposes the proud but gives grace to the humble. Humble yourselves, therefore, under the mighty hand of God so that at the proper time he may exalt you.

From this passage, leaders possess, at least, the following attributes:
- They 'shepherd the flock'. Here is a direct encouragement to lead as a shepherd, following the example of Jesus. They care about the progress, safety and welfare of the people they lead.
- They do not work 'for shameful gain'—that is, not out of selfishness or by using questionable methods. In chapter 2, I argued that as Christians we should concentrate on the 'inputs' to our jobs. Here is one. If you are a true leader, then you focus on leading and serving, leaving the outcome (any increase or bonus) to the Lord.
- They lead by example. Human beings are born imitators. This is one of the ways in which we learn from our parents. It is probably the *most effective leadership technique available to us* and Peter calls upon the leaders of the church both to lead by example and, by implication, to follow the example of the great Shepherd.
- They work 'eagerly, not domineering'. Enthusiasm is infectious and this is what Peter is recommending. Show yourself eager to practise servant leadership. Domineering behaviour does not fit the personality of a servant leader such as Jesus. You must resist any

temptation to be dictatorial. Rather, you should show a spirit of eagerness and, as we see next, humility.

• They work 'with humility'. We have already seen that Jesus was prepared to wash his disciples' feet. The same is true of Moses who was one of the greatest leaders who has ever lived. Yet notice how he is described: 'Now the man Moses was very meek, *more than all people who were on the face of the earth*' (Numbers 12:3, emphasis mine). How easily we become proud and then arrogant, especially if we rise to senior positions. This is the time when it is most necessary to think no more highly of ourselves than we ought (Romans 12:3). It is important to remember that whether you are the cleaner or the chief executive of a major company, you are a sinner saved by grace, bought with a price and that your position is always owing to God's grace, not your competence (nor lack thereof).

Humility will produce flexibility, not in matters of principle, but in your attitude to ideas, feedback and comments from your subordinates. Never be too proud to be open to *their* ideas even when they contradict yours. Another practical application of this is to heap praise on subordinates when your team achieves success. Never claim the praise for yourself. It is enough that the team that *you* led achieved something.

We have further teaching on elders in 1 Timothy chapter 3 and Titus chapter 1. From these passages, we learn more about the *character* of a biblical leader. It applies equally well to all leadership situations:

Therefore an overseer must be above reproach, the husband of one wife, sober-minded, self-controlled, respectable, hospitable, able to teach, not a drunkard, not violent but gentle, not quarrelsome, not a lover of money. He must manage his own household well, with all dignity keeping his children submissive, for if someone does not know how to manage his own household, how will he care for God's church? (1 Timothy 3:2–6).

From this passage, we add some other character attributes:

• *Above reproach* Here we have integrity observed. In another passage Paul pointed out that 'we aim at what is honourable not only in the Lord's sight but also in the sight of man' (2 Corinthians 8:21).

- *Morally pure* Our private lives *do* matter. People observe how we live and whether we can be trusted in our relationships. Why should they trust us if our wives or husbands cannot? Who will follow someone that they do not trust?
- *Sober-minded* That is a clear thinker. This is a part of vision but also means that a leader will avoid rash and foolish decisions. He will consider alternatives, think through every decision, taking as long as he has available.
- *Self-controlled* As we have already pointed out, everyone needs to be subject to control because we are all sinners. As you move higher up the corporate ladder, so external control becomes less frequent and, therefore, *self-control* becomes more important. I spent a large part of my business life working for a boss who was six thousand miles away. He could not check up on me and, to my knowledge, never questioned that I possessed sufficient self-control to be at work each day, at the appointed time and doing my job. Naturally, it goes deeper than that.
- *Attributes* such as 'respectable', 'hospitable', 'not a drunkard', 'not violent', 'gentle', 'not quarrelsome', 'not a lover of money' (for himself) are all self-explanatory and excellent qualities to develop if you wish to lead. Cultivate every one of them because you are unlikely to find these in any secular textbook. But I wish to highlight two further attributes which are especially important.
- *Able to teach* To do this, two qualities are essential: one, *knowledge* and two, the ability to *communicate*. You cannot lead if you have not prepared yourself for the task. There is no shortcut to studying and equipping yourself to do your job properly. We dealt with this earlier and it is especially true of the leader. The second quality, that of being able to communicate, has also been dealt with earlier. While it is important in everyone and key to good management, it is absolutely critical in a leader. Communication is not just about having ability as an orator (it is that) but more about being credible. People must believe *and* trust what you say. This takes us back to integrity and the

straightforward speech that we dealt with in earlier chapters. Make every effort to communicate in an honest, accurate and straightforward manner and, if possible, face to face.

- Finally, there is the matter of proving oneself in small things first. Paul invokes the same principle as Jesus did in the parable of the servants. Here Paul suggests looking at how a man manages his own home because if he cannot do that then he cannot lead the church, *nor, in my view, anything else*. Once again, contrary to secular thinking, our private lives do matter.

All of the above emphasize the love, humility and patience with which Jesus led. But we must never forget that he was an extremely strong character and would not tolerate any sin or hypocrisy. He had no hesitation in saying, 'But woe to you, scribes and Pharisees, hypocrites! For you shut the kingdom of heaven in people's faces. For you neither enter yourselves nor allow those who would enter to go in' (Matthew 23:13). This same statement is repeated several times. He was not soft on the money changes in the Temple. He used whips to remove them. He was enthusiastic about his Father's business. Humility or meekness must never be thought of as being weak, a 'wimp' or a lack of strength or resolve. Jesus himself was a carpenter or builder (very masculine occupations) and his immediate followers included all sorts of men, ranging from fishermen to tax collectors, from theologians to doctors. In today's world, we often project Christianity as a 'soft' faith suitable for bookworms or academics. Humble, yes, but soft, never.

Paul took the same position. Even Peter, whom he called a 'pillar' a few verses earlier, was confronted directly when he departed from the truth. 'But when Cephas came to Antioch, I *opposed him to his face*, because he stood condemned' (Galatians 2:11, emphasis mine). Paul was no coward and no weakling. We must be direct and straightforward in all our dealings with subordinates, colleagues and even our superiors. We must act with strength and determination.

The point is that a strong character will take strong action when necessary in support of the *cause* that he is leading. Every good leader will act decisively and with strength.

## Summary of Chapter 4

Jesus was the greatest leader of all time and we do well to follow his example. His leadership was in the style of a shepherd who leads by example from the front. Jesus also showed that we should serve those we lead. Jesus loved his 'sheep' even to the point of laying down his life for them. His leadership can be summarized in the following words: 'shepherding', 'servant leadership', 'humility', 'love'. Having said that, we also note that he was totally intolerant of those who practised evil and could act with resolve when needed.

Paul's leadership followed that of Jesus and is a useful example of how this style of leadership can be practised.

We are given substantial guidance on biblical leadership in the instructions of both Peter and Paul to elders. These are consistent with Jesus' leadership and Peter calls on us to follow his example.

## Case studies

### CASE STUDY 1

A well-known business leader invited me to visit his company and to see the extent and nature of its factories. He hired a helicopter and took me to some of the factories. As we walked around, I was astonished to see him greeting workers on the shop floor calling them by name, asking personal questions about their welfare and about their families. He clearly knew them even though this was the apartheid era in South Africa's history and they were all black. Then, as we left, I collected a huge box of the company's products which were to be a gift for my wife. This box could barely be carried by one man, but this leader insisted in carrying it (on his head!) to the helicopter. Here was an example of servant leadership and humility. He was prepared to do the lowliest of jobs and, in this case, it did not rob the company of his valuable time. Subsequently, I joined the company of which he was chief executive. Who wouldn't? I soon learnt that the corridors of this very large and successful company were full of stories about the humble, but very able, thirty-four-year-old chief executive. I read an article which claimed that he knew every one of the ten to twelve thousand people working in the factories of the company. I asked him directly if it was true. He blushed with embarrassment and laughingly said, 'No, I only know about half of them.' He knew five to six thousand of his employees by name and a good deal about them! Most of them were at shop floor level. This was a leader who cared about his people. (Was it *agape* love?) Senior executives told me that they often caught themselves wondering why they were doing extraordinary things for this man. I knew why and here I am writing about my experience some thirty years later!

His soft *personality* was not to be confused with a very able and decisive mind, a tough and determined will and a great ability to get things done, i.e. a fine *character*.

**CASE STUDY 2**
This case study illustrates the exact opposite of the previous one.

I knew the chairman of a very large and successful publisher. We enjoyed a relaxed and normal business relationship and did a fair amount of business together. Then I wanted to sell a product to this particular group and the chairman arranged for us to see one of his middle managers, together with his staff, to present our ideas. We all gathered in a conference room a few minutes before the meeting and were offered coffee or tea. Then a man entered with a beverage, added sugar to it, stirred it and put it at the head of the table where he sat quietly. After about ten minutes, a 'very important man' entered the room. Everyone stood up and the man sitting at the head of the table left the room. The 'very important man' then sat down on the seat that had been warmed for him and drank the beverage that had been cooled for him. Only then did he begin to lead the meeting.

Here was an example of what a good leader is not. Why? Put frankly, he was attracting attention to himself. He was feeding his ego and not serving anyone.

## Discussion questions

1. Identify a well-known leader and analyse his leadership qualities in the light of biblical principles.
2. Practise vision by analysing the likely *changes* in the environment in

which your organization operates. (You can make this your company, church, college, mission or any other organization that you care about.) Here is a hint—the following list gives some useful headings when considering the areas to analyse: political, economic, social, technological and competitive. From this analysis, summarize your 'vision' for the future of your organization.

# Work in difficult circumstances

During my forty odd years at work, I frequently attended events to celebrate long service or retirement. On these occasions, I listened to speeches about long, loyal service, rendered happily among wonderful people. I often listened to these speeches and wondered where I had gone wrong! Most of my time at work was peppered with problems, often accompanied by failures in human relationships.

## Problems at work

The reality is that most of us experience all sorts of problems at work. Sometimes a colleague seems determined to 'get' you. At other times, a subordinate ignores your requests. You may be undermined and misrepresented. Perhaps, one colleague just does not fit in and causes the team to fail. 'If only *he* were not here ...' goes through your mind. Does this sound familiar?

You may feel unable to cope. The job may be more than you can handle. Perhaps, a customer gives you a hard time and no matter how hard you try, you cannot satisfy him. Worse, he reports you to your superiors. Or, perhaps, your employer has fallen on hard times and is threatened with closure. Those in private practice or small business may be faced with the loss of clients or patients or customers. This may not be your fault but, nevertheless, it threatens your livelihood. Perhaps, you can identify with some of these typical problems.

The solution may call for some positive action on your part and this should be pursued vigorously. For example, if you feel inadequate for the task, you may need further training or, in a serious case, a change of job. If your practice or small business is not viable then, perhaps, an orderly closure is called for. You should always use prayerful common sense to resolve these situations. Providence is God's way of opening 'doors' for you and you should test every opening to see if God is at work in resolving the situation. But equally, he may not provide an opening, in which case, you must learn to 'be content with what you have, for he has said, "I will never leave you, nor forsake you"' (Hebrews 13:5).

## Significance of work

Despite difficulties, our jobs are very important to us. In fact, we tend to define ourselves by the work we do. When we meet someone for the first time, one of the first questions we ask is 'What *do you do?*' Sometimes, we get an answer that gives the person's 'position' such as 'I am a sales manager'; others will say, 'I am an accountant'; and others will say, 'I repair computers' and so forth. The difference between these answers is that one person sees his significance in the *status* of his job, while the other person sees significance in the *profession itself* (and is less likely to be concerned about his role or status within the organization). The third person sees significance in what he *does*. They all derive significance and security from their understanding of their jobs. Consequently, if a situation arises which threatens the individual's perception of his worth, then he will feel the problem keenly. This, in turn, leads to stress, one of the most common problems in the workplace.

One of the most hurtful experiences that we all encounter sooner or later is receiving negative feedback, even when this is supposed to be positive. We dislike facing up to our own shortcomings, real or as perceived by someone else. Sometimes, it is overt and addressed to the person concerned. Other times, it is behind the person's back but he is aware of it. And other times it is in public. How do we deal with such communications? Firstly, we have to face up to it and determine whether or not it is true. If it is false, then ignore it or place it before the Lord as Hezekiah did with his infamous letter (2 Kings 19:14). Leave it there. If, however, the criticism is true, it needs to be determined whether or not it is sinful. If it is sinful, then there must be repentance and this means turning entirely from it—that is, not committing the sin again. Sometimes, it will call for restitution. This may be in the form of an apology or even an undoing of the wrong committed. One of the great privileges of being a Christian is that we can obtain forgiveness. The world may not accept restitution or an apology, but God does and that is all that matters. Finally, if it is true but not a sin *and the person considers it a good idea to rectify it*, then all he need do is improve. It may be necessary to practise more self-control or discipline, learn new skills or gain more experience. Maybe there needs to be a change of attitude. Whatever is lacking, the person should make an effort to improve, if it is at all within his competence to do so. If it is not, or the person does not deem this work important for him to do, then ensure that others perform these tasks. This may be possible through re-arranging work with colleagues. But, in the worst case, a change of job may be what is needed. All of these should be relatively simple to determine and then to implement.

I shall illustrate some of these points from my own experience. For a considerable period my job was in the public eye because our company was in a high profile sector (Electronics and Telecommunications) and was listed on the stock exchange. Most of the time, the press reports were favourable (usually still inaccurate!) but, occasionally, something hurtful (and often erroneous) would be published. On one occasion, a leading newspaper reported that the managing director of our company had been charged with sexual harassment. Although I had a different title, it was easy for the public to read this as being me. I was naturally upset. The newspaper quickly discovered its error, wrote me a contrite apology and offered to put the matter right in as prominent a way as I chose. The true culprit was the managing director of one of our subsidiaries. I realized that if I allowed them to print an apology, it would more than likely raise the profile of the whole affair and the identity of the true culprit would be revealed in public. The entire matter had occurred several months earlier and had been properly dealt with. I was concerned about the man's family and about raising a now dead issue. I also knew that I was not guilty. God knew this too, and so did everyone who mattered to me. So, I accepted the private apology and let the matter rest. Later, I was pleased that I had done this for another reason. The real culprit became a Christian and then, not long after that, developed a brain tumour and died. I was pleased to speak at his funeral and not to feel that I had caused his sin, but rather his faith in a living Christ, to become public knowledge.

The most serious problem that we are likely to encounter is the loss of our job itself, whether by dismissal, retrenchment, closure of a practice, ill health or taking a legitimate pension. The cause is not the primary issue. It is the fact that the definition of *who we are* is destroyed. On a spiritual level, all of these problems threaten our security and often our sense of significance. These two emotions may lead to depression and a sense of meaninglessness. From my own experience and those close to me, I know the process. The person feels under pressure, unable to cope, and the resulting depression causes his output to drop, sometimes to a point that he cannot work at all. This makes him feel even more inadequate, making him do even less and so it goes on in a downward spiral. Eventually, he feels that he is at the bottom of a pit. Why is this? It is because people wrongly assume that they are defined by *what* they are and *how they perform* rather than *who* they are. How can the cycle be broken and how do people get back on top of things?

## The Fall

Firstly, we need to recognize that the basic problem is a result of the Fall. After the Fall, work became 'toil'. Weeds sprang up and made work a burden. Solomon put this neatly when he said, 'Then I considered all that my hands had done and the toil I had expended in doing it, and behold, all was vanity and a striving after wind, and there was nothing to be gained under the sun' (Ecclesiastes 2:11). Vanity is just another way of saying 'useless'.

## Perseverance leads to maturity

James shocks us by saying, 'Count it all joy, my brothers, when you meet trials of various kinds' (James 1:2). He goes on to explain that such trials teach us to be steadfast, leading to maturity. There is, therefore, a positive purpose even when things are difficult and spiralling out of control. Paul has recorded God's words to us, 'My grace is sufficient for you, for my power is made perfect in weakness. Therefore I will boast all the more gladly of my weaknesses, so that the power of Christ may rest upon me' (2 Corinthians 12:9). He goes on to be even more radical: 'For the sake of Christ, then, I am content with weaknesses, insults, hardships, persecutions, and calamities. For when I am weak, then I am strong' (v. 10). You are not the first person to encounter problems!

The point of all this is that God wants us to learn to trust him and not to rely on our own abilities. Under the circumstances that I outlined above, we are actually incapable of reversing the vicious cycle and making it into a virtuous circle in which we spiral upwards. We must yield to God and allow him to define our identity and give us significance and security.

Christian counsellors advise that when we are struggling as I have described, we should ponder and apply four doctrines to ourselves:

- Doctrine of propitiation: Jesus Christ died for our sins, demonstrating God's love for us while we were still sinners (Romans 5:8). This establishes our 'worth' despite our sins and feeling of inadequacy.
- Doctrine of regeneration: We are spiritually reborn which means that all our past, present and future actions are irrelevant in establishing who we are. Our new identity is 'in Christ'.
- Doctrine of justification: Based on the work of Jesus dying on the cross in our place, we are 'legally' declared 'just' even though we deserve nothing. God sees us (and other Christians should do the same) clothed in the righteousness of Jesus, not as poor broken human beings.
- Doctrine of reconciliation: Our broken relationship with God is re-established, not on the basis of what *we do* but on what Jesus *has done* for us. It also establishes a basis for us to be reconciled to our fellow human beings.

## Significance and security lie in Christ

The basic cure lies in redefining our sense of significance and security. We must learn to give an entirely different answer to the question: who am I? We are sinners saved by grace, bought with a price and a new creation in Christ. And what a price! God considered us valuable enough to send His only begotten Son to die for us (John 3:16). How valuable does this make us? Consider the Bible's record: 'You are not your own,

for you were bought with a price. So glorify God in your body'
(1 Corinthians 6:19–20).

God chose what is low and despised in the world, even things that are not, to bring to
nothing things that are, *so that no human being might boast* in the presence of God.
He is the source of your life in Christ Jesus, whom God made *our wisdom* and *our
righteousness* and *sanctification* and *redemption*. Therefore, as it is written, 'Let the
one who boasts, boast in the Lord' (1 Corinthians 1:28–31, emphasis mine).

This passage pinpoints the very issue which leads us to find our value in
our work—our pride. We want to boast about *who we are* or *what we are*
or *what we do* or have *achieved*. God says that what we are is to be found
in being what Christ *makes us*, namely, *wise* in biblical wisdom,
*righteous* through Christ's righteousness, *saved* though Christ's death
and *holy* though Christ's holiness. These are things worth boasting
about!

Elsewhere Jesus sets out our importance as human beings by means of
some very comforting comparisons. 'Are not five sparrows sold for two
pennies? And not one of them is forgotten before God. Why, even the
hairs of your head are all numbered. Fear not; you are of more value than
many sparrows' (Luke 12:6–7).

How do we apply this in practice? Whenever we are tempted to despair
and to feel threatened or useless, we should return to these passages. We
should seek to redefine who we are in spiritual terms, realizing that our
self-perception and the perception of all other people is not of any real
significance. During much of my working life, I was in the public eye.
This meant frequent newspaper and magazine reports. In fairness, most
were positive (usually wrong!) but sometimes they were cruelly wrong
and hurtful. Looking back, it does not matter now. It did not matter then
either. It is God's view of us that matters. How does He see us? As
believers, He sees us always as clothed in the righteousness of Christ.

In all the many problems that I encountered in my work, I can single
out three major problems, all of which led to me changing my job. All
three were traumatic in many ways. The amazing long-term outcome of
all three was an enormous improvement in my position. God did not fail

me. I hasten to add that this may not always be the case, but what we must learn is the truth set out above, namely, that his grace is *always* sufficient, whatever the outcome. Sometimes we end up in a worse position, but God gives the grace *to live with that situation as well*. Trust him.

If your problem is severe and you cannot break the vicious cycle leading to depression, then, by all means, seek professional help and even the use of medication. God in his universal grace has provided us with medical and psychiatric science. We should use these provisions of his love for us. What we should not do is turn to atheistic psychology which denies biblical truth.

## Summary of chapter 5

Ever since Adam sinned, work has been fraught with problems which will cause stress. The worst case often appears to be leaving a job. The reasons are not important. In all instances, these problems may make a person feel worthless. Stress may lead to anxiety and even depression. The cure is to find our significance and security in Christ, not in ourselves. We are sinners bought with a price. This makes us all of considerable value, regardless of our job.

### CASE STUDY

In one of our companies, a senior executive had been through a stressful period both at home and at work. He found himself spiralling viciously downwards in the circle described above. He said that he felt as if he was at the bottom of a pit and could not escape. No amount of talking and persuading helped. Logic was not the problem, feelings were more important. Despite this, the Bible says that the truth will make us free. His doctor (a Christian) wisely used medication but advised the services of a counsellor. His church referred him to a professional Christian counsellor who quickly had him back at work and functioning well. How did this happen?

The first lesson he had to learn was that he was defining himself in terms of his position and his performance but not according to the Bible's teaching. The counsellor taught him the four doctrines mentioned in this chapter in a loving and concerned manner, getting him to shift them from being theoretical truths, which he already knew, to real practical truths by which he could live. Patience and concern overcame the emotional barriers. The story has a happy ending. His performance thereafter was stellar!

### Discussion questions

1. Can you identify a period in your working life when you experienced stress? How did it end?
2. Consider the four doctrines outlined in this chapter and suggest practical ways in which these can be applied to stress in your work environment.

3. Imagine losing your job. What would be your greatest concerns? Why?
4. List the passages from the Bible that will help most in carrying you through difficulties. Try to memorize them or, at least, know where to find them easily.

# The Christian in a public company

Some of my readers will be in management, accounting or auditing roles in companies that are listed on a stock exchange. They will face additional challenges as they seek to apply biblical principles when doing business in the public eye.

With apologies to those in positions in a listed company and for the benefit of readers who are not knowledgeable about these matters, but wish to find out, we shall look at how stock exchanges function and what drives them.

## The stock exchange

A stock exchange is a supposedly 'free' market where capital can be raised by companies and where existing shares can be traded easily. In order to do this intelligently, the directors of the companies involved are required to present information about their businesses so that the public may make an intelligent assessment of the risk before purchasing or selling shares. There is nothing wrong with that in theory. Problems arise when companies fail to present an absolutely fair and accurate account of the past or prediction of the future even if the intention may not be to mislead. Clearly, any attempt by directors to present a false view of the prospects of the company is simply a misrepresentation and is 'bearing false witness'. In some cases, the public is given good information, but does not study or understand the material. Either way, the public may not base its trading on sound information, turning it into a *gamble,* which we classified as a non-legitimate source of wealth. This problem may be more true of individual investors but sometimes it also creeps into the behaviour of the 'institutional' investors, i.e. the mutual funds, insurance companies or pension funds. These investors control most of the movement of cash in any stock exchange. A large number of small transactions is also done by the public, often on a 'day trade' basis, buying and selling as soon as a gain is made and quite regardless of the underlying value of the share. In one sense, these traders are beneficial because they make the exchange more of a genuine market which is driven by many investors. But, on the other hand, their trading habits are seldom based on sound information. They merely follow the prevailing market which, as we shall see, is sometimes driven by itself and not always by facts or predictions. Consequently, when a share price is rising, everyone buys it simply because it is rising. This forces its price even higher, while ignoring any logic which may indicate that it is overpriced. Then something triggers a reduction in the share price and a suicidal 'lemmings rush' commences with everyone dumping the shares as the price tumbles, causing it to drop even faster. It becomes a gamble with 'investors' on the rising or falling markets playing the familiar game of chicken (the first person to lose his nerve and yield is said to be 'chicken'). This reduces share trading to gambling.

## Institutional investors

Institutional investors employ an army of 'investment advisors', 'share pickers' and 'asset managers'. These people investigate the companies and invest others' funds mainly in listed shares. They are trained to do financial analysis and determine the value of any share. Many do a good job and, in addition to looking at balance sheets, cash flow and other historic financial data, will sometimes investigate the market, the company's position in this market, the quality of management, technology, marketing expertise and so forth. The best managers will act on this data and ignore the wild movements described above. However, all too often 'investment science' is ignored and investors merely follow the market up and down, contributing to the unstable situation described above for the day trader. Their behaviour is driven by the realization that few investors admire an asset manager who does a thorough analysis and determines the correct price for a share when every other asset manager is simply buying in a rising market and selling in a falling market, showing wonderful 'paper' returns. This behaviour is driven by the excessive greed which pervades this industry. Asset managers receive massive bonuses (often seven figures) for beating a benchmark return (usually the average of all funds), even when the shares go down. They simply blame the market and provided that they lose less than others, they get a bonus. So doing worse than his competitors endears an asset manager to no one. They tend to follow one another, trying to buy earlier and sell later, thereby squeezing the maximum increase out of any share and minimizing any loss. Under these circumstances, the share price has little to do with the quality of the company.

What suddenly causes a share price to escalate or drop and trigger this whole unstable situation? Sometimes, it is genuine, valid news such as a new chief executive in the company, a technological breakthrough or some external news such as war, a hurricane or change in national politics. Often, it is some rumour which emerges from a company and which, rightly or wrongly, sparks a rising share price or a drop. All of this gives rise to huge pressure for a company continually to produce good news (or good rumours), which is usually code for rising profits, sales or number of customers, sometimes regardless of whether this is true or not.

## Greed

All of the above introduces another incentive for greed. In most listed companies, the senior executives are given the 'option' to buy shares based on the share price when they join the scheme and are entitled to sell these shares at a price which is hopefully higher at a subsequent time. These 'share options' can generate massive gains if the share price escalates a great deal between the time of taking the option and selling the shares. Consequently, managers focus on the share price and will sometimes do *anything* to trigger a rise. Under these circumstances, decisions may be made which favour share price rises, accounting standards may be compromised or reports falsified. In late 2001 several examples of such distortions received widespread media coverage. Enron, and their now defunct auditors Arthur Anderson, WorldCom and Tyco had found ways of presenting financial data which misled the investing public and the banks. So large was the deception that when the collapses came, records for bankruptcies were broken! It is worth noting that nine out of ten investment advisors were still advising investors to buy Enron shares a week before the collapse! *Fortune* magazine named Enron 'America's Most Innovative Company' for six consecutive years! The entire castle of cards was built on massive greed by the executives. Worse still, it is now clear that asset managers were trading in the shares without understanding the company and, doubtless, earned big bonuses for their great skill! CNN 'Money' of 25 May 2006, reporting on one of the ensuing court cases over the Enron affair, stated, 'Over sixteen weeks, the government presented twenty-two witnesses, including former top executives, who testified that Skilling and Lay fostered a culture that put the company's image and stock price above everything else, *at any cost*.' (Emphasis mine.) Who lost? The investing public and pensioners, people like you and me. (Ignoring, of course, the lost credibility of the asset managers!) The temptation to manipulate the market has not stopped. According to the *Wall Street Journal* for the week ending 24 August 2007, Dell (the computer maker) is the latest company to report enhanced earnings of $150 million over a period of four years. This was at the request of senior managers anxious to raise their share price. They will not be the last.

In 1995 the company which I headed was listed on the stock exchange. It was a very successful IPO (Initial Public Offering) which was twenty times oversubscribed. In the presentations that I was required to make, I had difficulty answering one of the questions relating to my personal share options. I was not attuned to the assumption that the chief executive was expected to be driven by sheer greed, so I played down my modest option percentage. I tried to explain that I believed in doing the best job I could and would always act in the shareholders' best interest, not my own. My explanation clearly fell on deaf ears and no doubt our share price suffered! So be it.

The 'dotcom' bubble of the 1990s was driven by the same greed and totally illogical values ascribed to shares in the IT industry. Solid businesses, well managed and based on good honest conservative accounting, were despised. I know because I led such a company!

How does all this stand up to biblical principles?

The most glaring sin is greed. Peter had this to say, 'They have hearts trained in greed. Accursed children!' (2 Peter 2:14).

The second sin is the breaking of the ninth commandment. Twisting performance is blatant dishonesty. We must use every endeavour to communicate truthfully and accurately.

A frequently asked question is whether or not a Christian should 'play' the stock market. My view is that if this is on a 'day trade' basis in which one is merely gambling, the answer must be 'no'. It is not work and nor is it an 'investment'. That said, the stock exchange is a legitimate market in which capital is raised for businesses and in which buyers and sellers can trade shares. It is, therefore, perfectly legitimate to 'invest in the market' in much the same way as one invests in the bank. Instead of interest, one earns dividends and the value of the shares may increase, resulting in a capital gain. But a word of caution. We are always to be good stewards, including of our own money. I am totally opposed to making a one-off investment in the stock market, even if the investment is in a mutual fund with a large spread of shares. The reason is that the stock market is very volatile and as a whole moves up and down every day, sometimes by quite significant amounts. If the investment is made on a 'high' day, a lot of money may be lost before the value of the investment even returns to the price that was paid for it. The only way in which I ever advise people to invest (as opposed to gamble) in the stock market is over a very long time *with a fixed amount being invested every month*. This is probably what most people are doing without even knowing it. A pension (whatever form it may take) and any investment component of an endowment insurance policy effectively does just that. The reason why this occurs is because the investor gets the benefit of what is called 'Pound cost averaging' (or 'Dollar cost averaging' or 'Euro cost averaging' or whatever currency is used.)

I shall explain how this works. The same amount is invested each month in some fund based on shares listed on a stock exchange. This investment will buy 'units' related to the share prices prevailing at the time of the investment. Assume that the market has fallen and each unit is therefore 'cheap'. This means that if the same monetary value investment is invested every month, many more units will be bought each month than when shares were expensive. Then, when the market swings up again, there will be more units to *gain value* and hence an excellent return will be received. The converse is also true. When the market is high, fewer units will be bought so that when the market falls there will be fewer units on which to lose. It can be shown that, even if the market swings up and down and ends up where it started, an investor will have acquired more shares to grow in value on every upswing than he has to lose on, on the downswings. Amazing but true. In summary, a constant monetary value invested every month in a stock exchange over a very long time (decades) is a good idea—*but never a one-off investment.*

## Summary of chapter 6

Using the stock market as a source of raising funds is quite justifiable but not as a gambling casino. All gambling (which is based on greed and avoids work) is outside of the biblical economy.

The need for a company to produce a continuous stream of 'good news' creates the temptation to lie about performance. This breaks the ninth commandment. The stock exchange, and to some extent the senior executives in listed companies, are tempted to selfish greed. Senior executives in listed companies face the dilemma of doing what is best for the company (their stewardship duty) or doing what boosts the share price in the short term.

The stock exchange is a good place to invest a regular amount each month over a very long term, using the 'principle of Pound cost averaging' but never for a one-off investment.

### CASE STUDY

You are the chief executive of a listed company. You are selling an asset (for example, an unwanted machine) and you will be paid in a year's time. It is not income and hence will not show up in your profits. The payer has no preference as to how he pays you; you can have him pay you a higher price in a year's time or he can pay you a lower amount plus interest. For the sake of illustration, assume that the basic amount is £100,000 and that a reasonable interest rate is 10 per cent. The total in a year's time would then be £100,000 plus interest of £10,000. Alternatively, he simply pays you a capital sum of £110,000 in a year's time. What do you choose?

### Discussion

If you choose to have him pay you the larger amount as *capital* in a year's time, there is no impact on profit. Hence, you will also pay no tax on the incoming cash although your bank balance will rise by the full amount of £110,000. The value of the company's assets will rise by £110,000 but this is unlikely to affect the share price as, in all probability, other factors will be used by the market to determine the share price.

If, however, you elect to take the capital sum as £100,000 plus interest of £10,000, then your profits will rise by £10,000 and your tax bill by about £3,000. Your bank balance will, therefore, only rise by £107,000, as will your assets. This option is actually worse for the company as it does not retain as much cash, although the taxman will be delighted. However, your profits after tax will rise by £7,000.

The most common determinant of the share price is the Price-Earnings (or PE) multiple. This number is multiplied by the profits (after tax) per share to yield the value of one share. So, if a company makes a profit (after tax) of £1 per share and the PE is 10, then the share price will be £10. The PE is determined by many factors such as the attractiveness of the market, growth, perceived quality of the company, etc. Unless any of these factors change, the PE will remain fairly steady in the short to medium term. Let us now see how the two options mentioned above will affect the share price.

We have already said that taking the higher amount later will probably not affect the share price (although it should!) but the second option will raise the profits (after tax) by £7,000. If the PE is 10, then the value of the company will rise by 10 x £7,000 = £70,000. You have increased your shareholder's value by £70,000, which is less than the £110,000 that you collected. If, however, the PE is 20, then the gain would be 20 x £7,000 = £140,000 even though you only banked £107,000, none of which has anything to do with the value of the asset sold!

This case is based on a real decision that I had to make.

### Discussion questions

1. In the case study above, which option would you choose?
2. What are the ethical issues if you select the second option?
3. Are share options wrong for a Christian businessman?
4. How would you distinguish between 'reward' and 'greed'? Can you base your answer on biblical considerations?

# Preparing for pension

## Retirement

I originally thought of calling this chapter 'The Christian after work' but did not do so because there is no such thing as 'after work' for a Christian. We may go on pension. There is, however, no biblical justification to stop working, unless you happen to be a Levite and work in the tent of meeting, in which case, you would retire at fifty, but then become a guard (Numbers 8:24–25). This is the only reference to retirement in the Bible.

The key issue is that the work ethic does not cease to apply at the age of sixty, sixty-five or even seventy. Remember the basis of the work ethic, namely, that we are image bearers of a working God. It is true that we also work to support ourselves but this is not where it started and nor is it the whole definition of work. God worked six days in creation and rested the seventh. We are commanded to do the same, unless our health prevents us from so doing. Women who have spent a large part of their lives as homemakers know full well that there is no such thing as retirement for them. Why should it be different for men?

There are other references in the Bible which are especially applicable to this situation: 'For even when we were with you, we would give you this command: If anyone is *not willing to work*, let him not eat. For we hear that some among you walk in idleness, *not busy at work*, but busybodies. Now such persons we command and encourage in the Lord Jesus Christ to do their *work* quietly and to *earn their own living*' (2 Thessalonians 3:10–12, emphasis mine). As I pointed out before, Paul was not suggesting that anyone should starve to death. This would have been in sharp contradiction to his concern about these matters. No, he was emphasizing the need to work and not to be *idle* or a *busybody*. This gives us a further hint as to why we should continue to work into 'old age'.

How do we apply this in our culture which is structured around relatively early pension and 'retirement', lasting perhaps twenty to thirty years after we leave our income earning jobs? Retirement conjures up images of golf, fishing, more golf, cruises, gardening and reading. Is this wrong?

Assume that you have been able to save sufficient money during your working life to give up your income earning job and stay at home or do something else. This is commendable and I am not suggesting that anyone should cease this practice, although I would suggest that you go immediately to the next chapter and review a Christian's *attitude* to wealth. You cannot place your trust in the 'nest egg' that you have accumulated, even if this is a state pension. Ask anyone who lived in Germany prior to 1939 or Zimbabwe in 2007.

For those on pension the question, therefore, becomes, 'What should I do with my life now that I do not need to work for a living?' The Bible is plain: *continue to work.* True, you may choose to do something very different from your previous job. You may choose to embark on some project which keeps you busy and has some value to you or society. Work is always *service.* You may choose to get involved in Christian service or so-called charitable work. You may concentrate on homemaking together with your wife. (Whoever said that homemaking was reserved for women?) The opportunities are endless. The point is that you should not be idle and not be a busybody (2 Thessalonians 3:10–12). Naturally, you may adjust your working hours so that you do spend more time on the golf course and less in an office, if you go to an office at all. You may also give yourself more holiday time. But you must continue to *work.*

This is sound practical advice because it comes from the Bible. I am assured by my son who is an actuary that statistics show that men who 'retire' and have no meaningful work to do other than going fishing, playing golf, and so on, die soon. We are created to work in a meaningful way even if the meaning is no longer to earn a living. By exercising the mind in a meaningful job, you also greatly reduce your risk of suffering from Alzheimer's or some other brain disease.

Another group of people 'go on pension' from full and meaningful jobs and struggle with the dramatic change in lifestyle. Consider some of the problems faced by them:

## Loss of significance

As we have already seen, some men and women define themselves in terms of what they did or the position they once held. Suddenly, they feel they have no authority, no support systems, no large office, no secretary, no significance, their lives have become meaningless and they are not accustomed to doing menial work which may be a necessity in their new role. (I even cook, occasionally.) This life-changing shock is hard to accept and some people are unable to adjust to it. The key is to return to chapter 5 where we discussed the true basis of our significance. We are not defined by our jobs but by who we are in God's eyes, namely, sinners bought with a price, the price being God's only Son. He never saw you as a company director, or as a messenger, but as a sinner clothed in the righteousness of his Son, Jesus Christ. All that matters is how God sees you. The view of neighbours, friends and even family does not really matter.

## Inadequate income

Sadly, a great many people will find themselves without sufficient income to make ends meet in their senior years, especially if one partner needs special care or medical support. The simple answer to this problem is to find a job, if that is possible and one's health permits. Failing that, the biblical approach is to call the extended family together and develop a plan (1 Timothy 5:8). In all of these cases, Jesus' comforting words about our material needs should not be forgotten: 'Your heavenly father knows that you need them all' (Matthew 6:32).

I shall now focus my attention on those who have not yet reached their pensionable age and advise them on how to plan to be able to support themselves when they no longer work to earn a living. Remember that Paul taught that it is our duty to provide for ourselves and our families (1 Timothy 5:8).

Many people who have jobs will have some sort of pension scheme (I use the term loosely) provided by their employer. This may or may not be sufficient to live on once they terminate their normal jobs and they may need to do some calculations or take professional advice. In all cases, remember that good *stewardship* calls on us to provide the most we can but *faith* teaches that our security does not and, never can, rest in this provision. We need always to be trusting God, despite having taken responsible action. Let me illustrate from my own life. After going on pension, I moved from South Africa to England. My pension is earned in South African Rands, but I spend it in English pounds. The exchange rate has declined by over forty per cent since I moved, reducing my pension significantly. To make matters worse, the company administering a large portion of my pension has gone into liquidation and I do not know if my funds will be lost. I know of others who have lost pensions in the UK and the USA. From time to time, financial institutions and banks go bankrupt and pensioners may lose their savings. No security here!

## Pensions

Before proceeding, and with apologies to those in the financial industry, I shall briefly explain so-called 'pension plans'.

There are basically two types. One is a genuine pension provided by an employer. It will probably be referred to as a 'defined benefit plan' or 'final income plan'. These plans pay a pension which is based on an employee's final income and years of service with the company, *regardless of what has actually been paid in or how well the fund has performed*. If the fund has been well invested and the amount in the fund exceeds what is needed to pay a pension, then we say the fund is 'in surplus'; but this may not translate into a higher pension. The pension is simply safer. However, in recent years, owing to stock market collapses and poor investments on the part of the asset managers (see chapter 6), many pension funds are 'under funded'—that is, they do not have enough cash to pay their pension obligations. In the UK, the aggregate 'under funding' by the major company pension funds is variously estimated at £50 billion to £100 billion. A similar situation occurs in the USA and other countries as well. It is, therefore, a major problem and is likely to affect many readers. Pensioners and even employees who are still to go on pension are, therefore, at risk and may not be paid the pension they expect. In many cases, all is not lost because these funds are underwritten by the company itself, i.e. the employer will pay in if necessary because a true pension is at the *employer's* risk. But what if the employer cannot pay or has already gone bankrupt? This has happened in many cases, leaving pensioners with reduced pensions or even lost pensions.

The second type of scheme is known as a 'defined contribution scheme'. It is sometimes called a 'provident fund' or an 'annuity' or 'superannuation' and in the USA a '401K'. This is really a savings scheme in which what is paid in, plus growth (or loss), plus dividends and interest will simply be paid back once a person goes on pension. Whether or not the employer contributes or simply pays a higher salary and the employee pays more in is determined by tax considerations. We shall not concern ourselves with tax as this differs from country to country, although it is an important component and professional advice should be taken with respect to it. The positive side of this method is that the employee gets the full value of the fund and if the fund performs well, he may end up with a very good pension. However, it is *the employee* who is taking the risk and, if the fund performs badly, he will get a lower pension. In recent years, both employers and staff have chosen to move to these defined contribution schemes because they have come to realize that the employer may not be able to guarantee the pension when the time comes. In this case, the employee ends up being at risk, so he may as well also enjoy any 'upside'. I suspect that apart from governments, true pension schemes are dead.

If you think that your employer's scheme will give you a sufficient income when you become a pensioner, then you may relax and wait until the time comes to enjoy your pension. However, you need to do some calculations because in most cases it will not. How much should you be putting away? We can work that out together. Suppose you work for thirty years and think that you will live for thirty years after you go on pension. Ignoring any growth in your savings and assuming that you want the same income on pension as you have received throughout your life, then it is very simple to see that you will need to save half your income when you are working. You live on half now and then the other half during the other half of your life. But this is a ridiculous case serving only to give us the upper limit of 50 per cent of your income. Now suppose that you think that you will live for only twenty years after you go on pension, then you need save only two-thirds of half your income or about 33 per cent. But, at that time, most likely you will have paid off your house, have no need to save for a pension, possibly have no children dependent on you and possibly plan to live in a smaller house. You may want an income of only about half the average of your previous income. Then you need to save only about 17 per cent of your salary. Inflation will require you to save slightly more but you can also expect growth in your fund so that you probably need to save about 15 per cent of you typical income, *provided that you do so all your working life.* If you start later, then you need to move to a higher figure and vice versa. Check what you are doing and, if necessary, top up. Naturally, this is a very rough guide but it is the figure most advisors will come up with and you can see why. Clearly, you may need less if you are expecting an inheritance or other lump sum and, maybe, you already own a lot of equity in your home. In fact, equity in your home is very important. I strongly advise people to pay off their home mortgage because this is the best way of accumulating an inflation beating asset. It is very much part of your retirement planning. When you need to, you can sell your family home and buy something smaller, putting the surplus into your retirement fund. Regrettably in the UK, paying off your mortgage has other negative results such as disqualifying you from certain benefits and raising your net assets at death which attracts inheritance tax. But these are other considerations and can be dealt with in various ways beyond the scope of this book.

It is important to note that some pension schemes come by other names. Do you have any endowment insurance? This is actually a savings scheme packaged with insurance that will produce a lump sum benefit at some time of your choosing, usually around when you plan to go on pension. In general, I do not advise endowment insurance for this purpose because a very large part of your premiums are paid in commission to the agent. However, there may be tax advantages, so this needs to be checked with an independent advisor—not the salesperson!

Suppose you decide to top up your pension plan? How best do you do it?

You will easily find a host of 'financial advisors' who will give you free advice and want to sell you amazing products that will make you rich some day. Beware of greed! You will be shown graphs of amazing performance and all you have to do is sign and start paying. I did that some forty years ago and guess what? I was the advisor and I believed all my own sales talk. During the last few years, I have been paid out all of these policies and none of them has produced results that even beat a post office savings account! This leads to rule number one. *Never take advice from anyone who stands to gain if you follow his advice.* If he is a salesman by any other name, use him as a salesman when you are ready to buy, but first seek independent advice and, if necessary, *pay for it.* For the record, commissions on endowment policies and some annuity schemes amount to a year (or more) of your premiums!

At this point, you should go back to Chapter 6 and read the section on 'Pound cost averaging' (or Dollar or Euro or any other currency). The point of this rule (call it rule two) is that you must *never put any lump sum* into the stock exchange but only use the stock exchange for very long-term investments with a more-or-less constant amount invested every month. Putting a *percentage* of your income into a stock market linked fund every month is fine. In fact, it is ideal for this purpose. The next question to ask is which fund? For this purpose, I once again recommend that you avoid the salesman no matter what his title. You can do most of what they do with a little common sense. I shall explain how. However, before proceeding, let me try to reduce all investments and insurances to their simplest forms (once again with apologies to those professionals in the industry).

## Insurance

Insurance allows you to pay a relatively small premium to an insurance company so that they take over whatever risk you want to transfer to the company. This is true for your home, your car, your life or your health. In the case of life insurance, the company takes over the risk of your dying sooner than the average life expectancy or becoming disabled and so forth. This is a good idea because for a relatively small premium you move serious risks away from yourself. Of course, you may pay for a very long time and never draw anything, but this is a blessing since it means that you are well and living! In short, it is a fair exchange and since there are many insurance companies to choose from, the free market works well. This is a good form of insurance and because it is simple and subject to considerable competition, the commissions are low. Most of the premium, therefore, goes into providing the insurance. However, do not confuse insurance with savings schemes which I shall deal with next.

## Savings

Basically, you can invest in one of two ways: one, at a fixed or semi-fixed return which is guaranteed and is usually in the form of interest or a dividend (which may have different tax treatments). Generally, this is in a bank, building society or 'thrift', government loans and so on. Or two, you invest in something that does *not* produce a guaranteed income or, even worse, you may lose your original capital as well. This may be property, shares, commodities, 'futures' and the like. While these are risky, they offer potentially higher returns and also tend to track inflation. We are currently in a period of stable prices but, not so long ago, we saw high inflation and this became a really important factor. It could happen again.

A stock market fund which spreads risk over a number of shares is variously called a 'managed fund', a 'mutual fund', a 'unit trust' or in Australia a 'superannuation fund'. Index funds are ones which purchase shares in the same ratio as the particular stock exchange index that you are buying, for example the 'FTSE' in England or the 'Dow' in the USA. Generally, they have outperformed the managed funds, although some managed funds would object to this statement. The problem is that you do not know which managed funds will outperform the index in future. Buying an index linked fund means that you will get a return which is the same as the growth in the whole market. Your investment is not guaranteed and you will find such a disclaimer on many of the web sites of the funds themselves. If the whole market collapses (as it did as recently as 1987 and 2001), your units will go down in value and the fund manager will simply blame the market for losing your money, even if he and all his colleagues are partly to blame for the collapse. Hence, the reason for Pound cost averaging.

How do you know which fund to invest in? You can get some idea about reputation and performance by reading the financial press over a period of time and perhaps by asking someone who will *not* get a commission from advising you. If you choose an index linked fund, you should look at the costs associated with the fund and check what is known as the 'loading'. Clearly, the lower the costs (or loading), the more of your money will work for you. The next problem is to find a low cost way of buying units in these funds. Try your bank. Otherwise, do some research on the internet. You want to avoid a broker who creams off a substantial percentage before your money ever gets to the fund. A 5 per cent upfront commission or a 0·25 per cent ongoing commission may not sound a lot but if your fund only produces a 7 per cent per annum gain (which is good long term), then you are giving a lot away. Key things to look for are commission costs, expense costs and reputation in the market.

## Combinations

There is nothing magical about the insurance or investment industry. The fancy sounding products offered by this industry are simply a combination of various forms of *savings* and *insurance* components as described above. The 'recipe' or mix may vary from product to product but the basic ingredients remain just the two mentioned above. So why pay someone else to mix your recipe if you can do it for yourself? There *is* a good answer. If you need something special or if you really do not have the skills to do it yourself, then buy a package. However, even then, think about it first because if you do, you will understand it better and make better decisions. Otherwise, buy the components yourself as described below.

My counsel is that the breadwinner in every family must take sufficient *level term insurance* to cover the vulnerable period of his life. The amount should be enough to produce an income that will replace his earnings for the critical period when he has children at school. We shall consider values in a case study below. If the breadwinner cannot afford the premiums on this policy when he is young, then he should 'insure his insurability', i.e. take insurance that will allow him to purchase the actual insurance at a later date without any further medical examinations.

Then, as a separate matter, commence saving. But, a word of caution and another rule, call it rule number three. *You can never borrow and save at the same time*. This may surprise you and you probably believe that it is good stewardship to be saving even though you have a mortgage and, perhaps, several other loans. Many people make this mistake. They borrow from the bank at for example 6 per cent per annum (or a lot more!) and then save (maybe with the same bank!) and get for example 4 per cent per annum. All they have done is made the bank richer by 2 per cent (or more!) by borrowing back their own money! *You are not saving until you have paid off all loans*, so do this as a matter of urgency. (If you are self-employed, check what loans you have accepted liability for, because the same argument applies).

The number one place to save is to clear all your short-term debts. Then concentrate on paying off your mortgage as fast as you can. This will give you an effective rate of return equal to the rate of interest that you are paying the bank (because you are *saving* this interest). In addition, because it is a *saving* and not an investment, it attracts no tax, making it even more attractive. Pause here for a moment. *If your best savings are to clear your debts, then even better is not to get into debt in the first place*. Most people will argue that they have no option for capital items such as a house or a car. Probably this is true for the house and, in any event, houses tend to appreciate, so owning one is generally a good idea, even with a mortgage. But think carefully before getting into debt for a car. You will pay a very high interest rate and own a *depreciating* asset. Never, ever use your credit to build up debts. The interest rates are horrific and the temptation to run up these debts is very high.

If you plan to save and cannot avoid taking out a mortgage, then try to use one of the modern mortgages which allows you to repay a variable amount each month and also allows you to withdraw any overpayment with ease. In South Africa, these are called 'access bonds'. In the UK, they are 'offset mortgages' or 'plus bonds' or 'draw down mortgages' or 'flexible mortgages'; and in the USA, nearly the same effect can be achieved by using a 'home equity loan' linked to a mortgage. By using one of these mortgages, you can pay off your mortgage at a higher rate than is necessary but you can easily withdraw cash from your mortgage if you run into the proverbial rainy day and have to draw from your savings. You, therefore, do not need to create a separate savings account. Incidentally, your bank will not be keen on you following this advice because, as illustrated above, they lose interest income. To my knowledge, only South African banks offer these mortgages as a standard and with the same interest rate for borrowing or repaying the mortgage.

If your mortgage repayment is such that the capital redemption portion (that is the part that pays off the debt) is of the order of 15 to 20 per cent of your salary, then theoretically you may not need any other saving for a pension *until the mortgage is fully paid*. But this may be cutting things too fine, so I advise that you also pay into a company scheme or invest in a mutual fund as set out below.

What about those who do not have mortgages, either because they have paid them off or do not own a property? I recommend finding a good *index linked mutual fund* and investing every month in this fund. Note that a *regular* and *similar* amount is vital if you want to enjoy the advantages of 'Pound cost averaging'. Alternatively, there are funds which are a combination of managed funds and index linked funds, properties, bonds, cash and whatever else is going. One of these might appeal to you.

What about investing a lump sum? Remember rule one is *never*, *ever* invest a lump sum in anything linked to the stock market. As an illustration, if a lump sum had been invested early in 2001, it would have lost 30–40 per cent of its value within the first two years. It would only have regained its original value by 2007! It will take very good performance to recover the loss and then still give a positive return within, for example, ten years. So what do you do? There are various schemes advertised called by exotic names or sometimes 'bonds'. They will guarantee your capital (so that you do not have the problem mentioned above) and then something like 50 per cent of the growth of a stock market index. Sounds good, but you can do this yourself very easily and get 100 per cent of the growth! Here is how: Take the lump sum and place it in the best long-term interest (or dividend) earning investment you can find which *will pay interest monthly*. This will usually be in a bank. Then have the bank use that monthly interest to buy units in the mutual fund of your choice. These monthly investments will give you 'Pound cost averaging' and will produce a good return even if the stock exchange bounces around. Only if the stock exchange goes into a protracted slide and does not recover before you want the cash will the results be poor, but never nothing. In reality, the long-term slide has never happened. The declines are always fairly sharp and then they produce substantial returns when the market recovers. The 2001 slide did continue until 2003 but even this is 'short' if we are looking at an investment lasting decades.

Readers who wish to study this subject further are referred to the works of Larry Burkett,[1] especially if they live in the USA.

## Summary of chapter 7

There is no biblical case for anyone to stop working because of age. It is, however, permissible to switch from earning a living to drawing a pension provided that you continue working in some meaningful way.

Should you end the earning period of you life with inadequate funds and are unable to find another income earning job, then your immediate family needs to consider ways of giving assistance.

For those who intend to provide an adequate income for their later years, savings are suggested which rely on 'Pound cost averaging' (or Dollar or whatever currency you use). This calls for a regular amount saved every month over a long period of time.

It is impossible to save and borrow at the same time. So, first pay off all debt, including your mortgage, preferably using one of the mortgages which allows you to have access to your money again if you need it.

### CASE STUDY

Suppose you are a father, thirty years old, earn £3,000 per month and have bought your own home worth £250,000. You borrowed £50,000 from your parents (which they probably do not want repaid) and have taken a mortgage for the balance of the purchase of the house. You have no other debt. Your wife stays at home to care for the children aged six and four. What insurance do you need?

We can assume that your children will need support for about the next twenty years, so you should buy sufficient short-term insurance to generate an income that will replace your *net* salary for that period. Should you die at any time during the twenty years, the only costs that will fall away are those associated with you, i.e. your food, transport, clothes, etc. Assume that, after tax, your income is £2,500 per month of which £500 is for your expenses. Your wife will, therefore, need an income of about £2,000 (after tax) per month but rising over the years to compensate for inflation. To generate this sort of income and completely use up the capital over the twenty years, she will need to invest about £400,000 if you died tomorrow. The worst case scenario must be able to cover your family's needs from the first day that you are not there to provide for them but, as the years pass by, the figure will decrease. For example, after ten years she will only need about £250,000. Consequently, you could buy life insurance for £250,000 for the full twenty years and £150,000 for just ten years. Clearly, you can calculate more finely than this and cover your life in five-year intervals, starting at £400,000 and decreasing by £50,000 every five years. However, after the twenty years, your wife will have nothing, so you need to keep some additional insurance policies running for the duration of your life to ensure that her ongoing financial needs will be met. How much should that be? Once the children are off her hands and the house is paid for, she may only need about £200,000 and even this can reduce in, for example, £50,000 amounts every five years. Another solution is to make sure that your pension continues after you die.

A word of caution. Your mortgage provider will no doubt want you to hold insurance for the value of the mortgage, i.e. insurance to an initial value of £200,000. Superficially, it would seem that this can be covered by your £250,000 insurance proposed above. But the mortgage provider will think differently and will want the mortgage paid off on your death, leaving your wife with too little to generate an income to live on even though she will own a house which has been paid off. You will, therefore, need to take out an additional £100,000 worth of term insurance in addition to the mortgage cover of £200,000 to give the family a reasonable cash income.

All of this assumes that your wife will never take an income earning job and that she gets no support from welfare or anyone else. To the extent that this is not true, you can reduce the amounts calculated above. On the other hand, you may have established a lifestyle which needs more than the £3,000 per month base that I worked on. You must do your own calculations but I trust that I have illustrated the principles.

## Discussion questions

1. What work do you plan to do when you end your income earning job? If you are in a group discussion, then have everyone share his plans for the encouragement of the group.
2. Consider your family finances. Are you borrowing and saving at the same time? If so, calculate how much you are losing by this practice. Is

this good stewardship? How can you change your financial structure to prevent this practice?

3. Consider all of your investments, insurance policies, pension and savings schemes. Are they meeting the criteria set out in this book? If not, what will you change?

4. What loans do you have? How can you pay them all off and stay out of debt thereafter?

## Chapter 8

# A Christian attitude to wealth

L ike most people, I worked for many years in paid employment and looked forward to the time when I could receive my very adequate pension and take life a little easier. More importantly, I wanted to serve the Lord in different ways such as by writing. I was well off and had no ambition to increase my wealth. But some remarkable opportunities arose and I found that I could gain considerably more assets if I continued to employ my business skills. The problem of my attitude to gaining even more wealth now became critical and put my theoretical views to the test.

You may be wealthy or poor but sooner or later you will need to face up to mankind's innate desire to have more wealth. How do you handle this matter? The Bible clearly anticipates wealth and does not condemn it as we have already seen. Instead, the Bible gives very specific instructions to the wealthy concerning their *attitude* and their *use* of wealth. As soon as it becomes greed, or a treasure or a means of security, it replaces God and becomes idolatry.

### The desire to be rich

It is worth noting that Paul also addresses those who 'desire to be rich'— that is, those who rightly or wrongly regard themselves as poor. 'But those who *desire* to be rich fall into temptation, into a snare, into many senseless and harmful desires that plunge people into ruin and destruction. For the love of money is a root of all kinds of evils. It is through this craving that some have wandered away from the faith and pierced themselves with many pangs' (1 Timothy 6:9–10, emphasis mine). It is clear that the love of money, not money itself, is the root of all kinds of evil. It is our *attitude* that makes a difference between greed and its opposite, which is contentment. The antidote to greed is generosity.

### Instructions to the rich

Paul addresses the *rich* with these instructions: 'As for the rich in this present age, charge them not to be haughty, nor to set their hopes on the uncertainty of riches, but on God ... They are to do good, to be rich in good works, to be generous and ready to share' (1 Timothy 6:17–18). Who are the rich? Millionaires, billionaires or middle class people living comfortably?

It is worth emphasizing the various points that Paul makes in this section:

Riches often lead to *haughtiness* or *pride*. This arises because we love to think that *we* generated the wealth. This is wrong, and so the 'rich' must work hard to remain humble. It will not come naturally. The second evil is *trusting* in riches instead of recognizing that our ultimate security is in God. We probably all know of people who have worked hard all their lives, did all the wise things to provide for old age and then found that their pension was worthless through no fault of their own. I gave some examples in the previous chapter. There is a huge temptation for all of us to see our security in the riches that we hoard for the 'rainy day' or our old age. This is not to say that we should not use every means to provide for those events. Paul called on each of us to provide for our families (1 Timothy 5:8). The issue is whether or not we *trust* in these provisions or recognize that our only true security lies in our position 'in Christ'. Jesus called the rich man who filled his barns and thought that all was well a 'fool' (Luke 12:20). Psalm 49 warns all who trust in their riches.

God provides all things for us to enjoy, including even the very riches which we accumulate (1 Timothy 6:17; Ecclesiastes 5:18–19). But we should never forget what we learnt in earlier chapters, that it is God who gives us the ability to generate wealth and all the benefits that wealth brings.

The rich are to use their wealth to do *good works*, to be *generous* and to *share*. Good works are often misunderstood in the Bible. Good works are those things that bring glory to God, especially through the spreading of the gospel and building up of the church. In other words, we are to contribute generously to God's work, which should include caring for the poor. Notice the details that Paul goes into concerning this matter in 2 Corinthians chapters 8 and 9. James also exhorts us to take practical action when we see a real need: 'If a brother or sister is poorly clothed and lacking in daily food, and one of you says to them, "Go in peace, be warmed and filled," without giving them the things needed for the body, what good is that?' (James 2:15–16). Those of us who have the means must act. The antidote to greed is generosity, as Paul points out in 1 Timothy 6:18.

How is this done in practice? Imagine you are rich. You wish to do all that Paul says and so you entertain all the appeals from missions, churches, charities and so on. Soon all your money has gone. If you are still young and healthy, you could go on working. But what if you cannot work for some reason? You now join the ranks of the needy and will be seeking assistance yourself. Surely, this is not what Paul intended.

My suggestion is that if you are in this position, you give generously from the *income* of your wealth but that you keep the capital intact so that your generosity can be long lived and you can leave something to your children and grandchildren. 'A good man leaves an inheritance to his children's children' (Proverbs 13:22). You should try to be creative in what to do with the *capital*. Here is an example of such. One of the needs of many ministries is for accommodation. This calls for large capital sums which are then tied up so that they are not available for pursuing the aims of the ministry. You can finance the purchase of a building and offer the accommodation to the ministry at a reduced rental—even free? In this way, you retain the capital for future use or inheritance and, because property generally follows inflation over the long term, the value of the capital will be protected. Your capital is also put to good use which is good stewardship.

The Bible has a lot more to say to the rich, so we look at a few further exhortations.

They must not be *covetous* (Exodus 20:17). It is a human weakness that however much we may have, we always want a bit more. 'He who loves money will not be satisfied with money, nor he who loves wealth with his income; this also is vanity' (Ecclesiastes 5:10). Occasionally, I have set time aside to calculate what I have accumulated. There is nothing wrong with doing this and, indeed, good stewardship probably encourages it. Furthermore, without this knowledge, I do not even know how much I can give away. But I have always found myself being tempted in two ways: one, to be proud of what I (I?) have accumulated and two, I have always discovered that it was just a little short! The opposite is found in Paul's exhortation to be content with what we have. 'Now there is great gain in godliness with contentment' (1 Timothy 6:6).

Jesus taught us not to 'treasure' wealth—that is, make it something that we value highly. 'Do not lay up for yourselves treasures on earth, where moth and rust destroy and where thieves break in and steal, but lay up for yourselves treasures in heaven, where neither moth nor rust destroys and where thieves do not break in and steal. For where your treasure is, there your heart will be also' (Matthew 6:19–21). Making anything a 'treasure' robs God of the worship that we owe him. It is breaking the first commandment.

We are to be good stewards. The meaning of stewardship is 'to look after the property of someone else'. We must remember that everything that we enjoy actually belongs to God. We must, therefore, be careful even with what we consider to be our own. We must not squander our assets nor use them in 'riotous living'. We are to act responsibly, making sure that we have fulfilled our obligations to provide for ourselves and our families, always avoiding the temptation to *trust* in our assets. 'But if anyone does not provide for his relatives, and especially for members of his household, he has denied the faith and is worse than an unbeliever' (1 Timothy 5:8).

Finally, we should remember the source of all riches. Read the admonition given to the children of Israel: 'And when the LORD your God brings you into the land … with great and good cities that you did not build, and houses full of all good things … and cisterns that you did not dig, and vineyards and olive trees that you did not plant—and when you eat and are full, then take care lest you forget the LORD' (Deuteronomy 6:10–12). It continues a few chapters later, 'Beware lest you say in your heart, "My power and the might of my hand have gained me this wealth." You shall remember the LORD your God, for it is *he* who gives you power to get wealth' (Deuteronomy 8:17–18, emphasis mine). In the New Testament, Paul reminded us to be thankful, 'giving thanks always and for everything to God the Father' (Ephesians 5:20).

## Summary of chapter 8

It is not wrong to be rich, nor virtuous to be poor, but greed is a sin for both the rich and the poor. God has given us 'all things to enjoy'.

Riches must not lead to pride but rather to generosity and good works. We must not trust in riches nor make them a treasure. We are to be good stewards of our assets. True gratitude for what we enjoy comes from never forgetting who has given us the ability to earn anything.

### CASE STUDY

I know a couple who grew up in apartheid South Africa with first-hand experience of being destitute. Today, many years later, both husband and wife are fine Christians and relatively comfortable. Both still work hard as they have done for many years and today they own a home which is free of any mortgage, drive two cars and have no debt. They could easily attribute their status to their hard work—which in a very commendable sense it is—but they have never forgotten who it is that *enabled* them to prosper (Deuteronomy 8:17–18). They are generous, helpful and use all their free time to serve the Lord and others. We give thanks for three meals a day and I am sure we are sincere each time. But ask my friend to give thanks for a meal. It is so obviously different. With sincerity and emotion that is moving, he always prays, 'Lord, thank you for the *privilege* of another plate of food.'

### DISCUSSION QUESTIONS

1. On the one hand, Paul teaches stewardship and specifically that a man must provide for his own family (1 Timothy 5:8) but, on the other hand, we are not to trust in riches (1 Timothy 6:17–19). Discuss practical ways in which you can maintain a balance between these two truths.
2. Is God on the side of the poor?
3. Who are the rich?
4. In what practical ways can we avoid covetousness and greed?
5. Should Christians participate in competitions such as 'Survivor', 'Who wants to be a Millionaire?' and 'Greed', for example?

In addition to those books listed as references, the following books are recommended for further reading:

**David Oliver,** *Love work, live Life* (Authentic Media, 2006).

This is an easy read and a helpful book.

**David Chiltern,** *Productive Christians in an age of guilt Manipulators* (Tyler, TX: Institute For Christian Economics, 1981).

I hesitate to recommend this book because it is written as a sarcastic rebuttal of Ronald Sider's books. I agree with his rebuttal, if not his style, and commend his dealing with most economic issues on a biblical basis.

**Alistair Mackenzie** and **Wayne Kirkland,** *Where's God on Monday?* (Colorado Springs, CO: NavPress, 2003).

This book deals with the wider definition of work that I have not covered in my book. It also deals well with the misconceptions of dualism, i.e. 'clergy' versus 'laity' or 'secular' versus 'spiritual'.

**Rodney Green,** *90,000 Hours* (Bletchley: Scripture Union, 2002).

This is a useful book in which Green roots his views in theology. Its unique feature is that it is written by a leader in public service.

## Message from the Chairman of 'The Good Company'

The Good Company must conduct itself with honesty, integrity and in an ethical way. This is essential if it intends to maintain the confidence of the communities that it currently operates in or will prospectively operate in. All employees, directors and officers of the company are required to comply with the standards laid down in this Code of Ethics. Appropriate disciplinary action may be taken where an individual has contravened this Code. While appreciating that persons and organizations outside The Good Company will follow their own conscience, we do expect our customers and suppliers to respect our Code and deal with us in an ethical manner.

Our policy is to abide by the law in all countries where business is conducted. Even if there is no prescribed law, rule or regulation covering a given situation, every employee is expected to do the right thing from an ethical point of view and to look after the interests, reputation and goodwill of the company.

From time to time, this Code will be reassessed to ensure that it addresses all aspects of the socio-economic environment in which The Good Company operates.

The Good Company accepts that 'honesty' and 'integrity' are absolute concepts which are summarized in one or more of the Ten Commandments.

N O T Goodenough
(Chairman)

### CODE OF ETHICS OF THE GOOD COMPANY

The Good Company is committed to high standards of conduct in carrying out its business. We have an obligation to our customers, suppliers, investors, employees and the community at large to manage our business in an ethical and legal manner.

*THIS REQUIRES THAT WE:*

- **Conduct** all dealings with our customers and suppliers with honesty and integrity;

- **Respect** the rights of all employees to fair treatment and equal opportunity, free from discrimination or harassment;
- **Know**, understand and comply with the laws, regulations and codes governing the conduct of our business—both domestic and foreign;
- **Work** for The Good Company with loyalty, diligence and efficiency;
- **Ensure** that all financial transactions are handled honestly and recorded accurately;
- **Protect** information that belongs to The Good Company, our customers, suppliers and fellow workers;
- **Avoid** conflicts of interest, both real and perceived;
- **Never** use The Good Company assets or information for personal gain;
- **Recognize** that even the appearance of misconduct or impropriety can be very damaging to the reputation of The Good Company and will, therefore, act accordingly.

### DEALING WITH CUSTOMERS AND SUPPLIERS

Customer-focused quality is the core value of The Good Company.

We have an obligation to deliver the products and services on time as they have been promised and to charge customers the agreed price, or where no price was agreed, a fair price. We must not mislead customers when selling products or services, nor must we knowingly supply them with a defective or dangerous product. A customer's decision to buy from us should be based on the merit of our product and service offered. A customer, or any of their employees, must not be induced to purchase from The Good Company through bribery, coercion or manipulation. We will apply the same treatment to our customers as we expect to receive from our suppliers.

Similarly, we have an obligation to treat our suppliers fairly. We should ensure that all approved suppliers are given the opportunity to compete for our custom, and provide them assistance in understanding and achieving our product and service quality requirements. The Good Company has an obligation to settle amounts due to suppliers within the agreed terms of trade.

Dealing with suppliers is an area where conflicts of interest, real or perceived, may arise. An employee engaged in buying on behalf of The Good Company must not be allowed to be improperly influenced in their choice of supplier. Employees may not accept gifts from suppliers on their own account except advertising items such as company diaries, calendars or other company embossed gifts that have no commercial value. All offers of other gifts should be disclosed to the employee's manager who may give permission to accept them or take them for the company to use depending on the circumstances. The total value of gifts accepted by an employee may not exceed 0·1 per cent of the recipient's basic monthly salary.

Entertainment such as lunches, dinners, sports fixtures, theatre tickets, etc. are permissible provided that the direct cost to the giver does not exceed 1 per cent of the recipient's basic monthly salary. It will be considered a serious breach of conduct if an employee solicits any gifts or other forms of inducement from a supplier. Any supplier receiving such an approach from a The Good Company employee should immediately report the matter to his manager, who should in turn inform The Good Company. The matter will be treated in the strictest confidence.

### BUSINESS CONFLICTS AND PERSONAL INVESTMENT

The Good Company respects the rights of employees to manage their personal financial affairs and to conduct other activities outside of normal working hours. However, a conflict of interest arises when an employee, or any member of his immediate family, has an interest in any business or property or an obligation to any person that could affect the employee's judgement in fulfilling his responsibilities to The Good Company. Accordingly, employees are required to refrain from any personal business—financial or other activity—that constitutes a conflict of interest. This includes having a substantial holding in, or a professional affiliation with, a company with which The Good Company does business or with which The Good Company competes.

The Good Company welcomes employees supporting The Good Company through direct investment and benefiting from its long-term prospects. If The Good Company is listed, the following information will apply. It is a statutory offence to deal in The Good Company shares (or any other type of quoted security) on the basis of unpublished price sensitive information—a practice known as 'insider trading'. Employees should, therefore, be very careful when dealing in The Good Company's shares. This caution should also be exercised in dealing in shares in companies with which The Good Company has either a direct or indirect relationship. This caution should further be extended to the divulging of such information to others who may take advantage of it. If you are concerned that your dealing in shares could be construed as insider trading, you should contact a director or The Good Company Secretary before buying or selling shares.

*ACCURACY AND COMPLETENESS OF ACCOUNTING RECORDS AND REPORTS*
Accounting records are relied upon to produce reports that are used by management and many parties outside The Good Company, including investors, suppliers, customers and the government. In addition to legal requirements, The Good Company has an obligation to prepare published financial reports in accordance with the relevant standards of accounting and to ensure that assets, liabilities, income and expenses are fairly stated. Employees are prohibited from producing or keeping false or intentionally misleading accounting records, even if these do not lead to their personal gain.

*EMPLOYMENT PRACTICES*
Employees constitute an important resource. It is the policy of The Good Company that all employees are treated fairly and equitably in accordance with the rules of The Good Company and the laws of the country. We strive to place employees in positions that are best suited to their capabilities and to provide an environment where they can develop their potential as an employee and individual. Relationships between people working together must be based on trust, loyalty and respect. In this regard, The Good Company is committed to a policy that protects employees from discrimination and harassment, and to operate in safe working conditions.

We will pay market related remuneration consistent with the effort and contribution that an employee makes towards the prosperity of The Good Company.

In the event of disciplinary steps being taken, The Good Company will treat employees with respect and fairness.

Notwithstanding all the above, The Good Company will be proactive in assisting disabled and disadvantaged people to work and compete with their fellow employees in an environment which is equitable.

Employees on their part will work with loyalty, diligence and efficiency, regarding The Good Company as an important component of our society. They will always work to advance the best interests of The Good Company as a whole and to strive to enhance the wealth of the shareholders.

### COMMUNITY ACTIVITIES

The Good Company strives to be a good corporate citizen and encourages its employees to do likewise. However, no employee shall use his position within The Good Company to unduly influence or force other persons or organizations to participate in the activities that he is involved in. Employees who hold public office or serve on commissions or advisory groups should be careful of real or potential conflicts of interest and be prepared to abstain from participating in any deliberations or voting on any issue that directly involves The Good Company, its subsidiaries or associates.

### POLITICAL ACTIVITIES

The Good Company seeks to make a positive contribution to the economic and social well-being of the communities in which it operates but not to become involved in politics. The Good Company does not offer any comment on the actions of political parties or make contributions to political parties or candidates. The Good Company respects the rights of individuals to join or support political organizations and will take steps to ensure that employees will not be intimidated, victimized or prejudiced for their political beliefs. However, we do not allow employees to be active in party politics by holding executive office in such organizations whether as an elected representative or official in any organization in which party politics is the aim of the organization, nor do we allow campaigning on behalf of a political party on The Good Company's premises.

### PROTECTING INFORMATION

Commercial and technical information relating to The Good Company's business is a valuable commodity and we must ensure that it is protected from loss, theft, inadvertent disclosure or misuse. Employees and the company will adhere to privacy laws in the countries in which the Good Company operates. Utmost care must be taken in handling company information that is confidential such as unique technical or product data, product costs, business plans and information relating to our company or our customers. Should this type of information fall into the hands of unauthorized persons or competitors, it could have an adverse impact on The Good Company or its employees. Avoid discussing company business with unauthorized persons, even close friends, neighbours and relatives; they may inadvertently pass on the information to others. Furthermore, you should not discuss sensitive matters, even with authorized persons, in public places.

Some of our business may be associated with work affecting national security, and here there are clearly defined laws and regulations governing the handling of such information. Protecting this information involves not only the proper handling of documents but restricting the disclosure of their contents to individuals who have a proper security clearance and a need to know.

We have established controls to ensure that no unauthorized person can access company information via our computerized information system. You should always observe the disciplines of systems access control and distribution and the handling and filing of computer reports. Should you become aware of any breach of The Good Company's computer systems security, you should immediately inform a member of the technical staff.

Public reports and announcements to the press are only to be made by authorized personnel.

The Good Company respects the right of its employees to

confidentiality of information concerning themselves. Our staff have an obligation to ensure that private and personal information of an employee is kept confidential and only released to authorized persons. We will not give information regarding an employee or former employee to outside organizations or individuals without the employee's permission, unless there is a legal requirement to do so.

The gathering of information relating to technical and commercial developments outside The Good Company must also be conducted ethically and legally. You should not obtain such information from competitors, customers or potential customers in a way that involves theft, bribery or coercion.

### COMPANY PROPERTY AND BENEFITS

You may not use, appropriate or divert The Good Company property for your personal use or benefit. Removal of The Good Company property from its facilities may be regarded as theft. No item of The Good Company property may be destroyed or materially altered without permission.

### TRAVEL COSTS

Employee travel is a significant factor in the cost of conducting company business. Any travel incentives earned on The Good Company travel are company property and will be used as The Good Company deems fit. Employees who travel at The Good Company's expense have the responsibility of adhering to company policies and assisting in the reduction of travel costs.

### OTHER EXPENSES

Expenses incurred in the conduct of The Good Company business must be reported promptly, accurately and comprehensively. No false claims should be made.

### SOFTWARE

Any form of software purchased for The Good Company must be used within the boundaries defined by its licence agreement. No pirated or otherwise illegal software may be used or sold by The Good Company.

*COMPLIANCE*

It is through its employees at all levels of the organization that The Good Company can practise and achieve the standards of business conduct to which it aspires.

It is the duty of each employee to act in accordance with this Code of Ethics. This includes the obligation to report any questionable activities to his manager, or to a director. Within the constraints of legal requirements, The Good Company pledges to keep confidential the identities of employees who submit such reports.

The rules set forth in this Code and other The Good Company policies and procedures will be enforced at all levels, fairly and without prejudice. Employees who violate these rules may be subject to disciplinary action in accordance with The Good Company policy. This could result in dismissal, restitution of losses, civil action or criminal prosecution.

Complete the questionnaire *Time use table* for the hours you spent in a *typical* week. Ignore holidays, sick time and any non-recurring time. Be careful not to double count, e.g. by including eating time in both essential life support and at work.

There are 168 hours in a week. Compare your typical hours with 168.

If you think you use more than 168 hours, then you have either discovered the secret of a longer day or you need to rework your numbers!

If, however, you come up well short of 168, then you have more hours to fill. This may surprise you but it is quite normal. Where are all these hours? Generally, they occur in 'wasted' time between activities such as waiting for the evening meal, waiting to go to bed, idle chatter, watching more TV than intended—even being too early for meetings. Check your life for these time wasters. Here are some other activities to check for more profitable use of time:

- When you arrive home from work and are waiting for the evening meal, you probably claim that it is time to 'unwind'. Do you really need to do *nothing* to unwind? Try doing something productive instead—like mowing the lawn or playing with the children. You will still unwind and could do something useful.
- You decide to go to bed but then allow time to pass doing nothing of any value. Time how long it takes you between the time you decide to go to bed and actually getting into bed. What do you accomplish in between?
- If you are waiting for a meal or for someone to arrive, try reading.
- You arrive too early at a meeting. Either use the time productively or improve on your timing. Some meetings are best arrived at late. I can hear the howls of protest! But think about some formal or business meetings where you can make no contribution in the early stages when minutes are being approved, etc. Naturally, if you can make no contribution at all (including voting), nor benefit in any way, then don't go at all!

## Time Use Table

| Item | Hours |
|------|-------|
| **1. Essential life support items** | _____ |
| Sleeping | _____ |
| Eating | _____ |
| Ablutions | _____ |
| Household chores, e.g. cooking, washing dishes, etc. | _____ |
| Attending to family finances, paying bills, etc. | _____ |
| **2. Work** | _____ |
| Normal hours at work | _____ |
| Average overtime per week | _____ |
| Travel to and from work | _____ |
| Work done at home | _____ |
| **3. Recreation** | _____ |
| Sport or keeping fit | _____ |
| Reading, including newspapers, etc. | _____ |
| Watching TV, Movies, DVDs, etc. | _____ |
| Gardening | _____ |
| Hobbies | _____ |
| Visiting friends, etc. | _____ |
| **4. Family** | _____ |
| With wife | _____ |
| With children/grandchildren | _____ |
| With other family members | _____ |
| **5. Church** | _____ |
| On Sundays | _____ |
| Midweek meetings | _____ |
| Committees | _____ |
| Work for the church/mission/charity, etc. | _____ |
| Entertaining/hospitality | _____ |
| Visiting, church related | _____ |
| **6. Study** | _____ |
| Formal towards a further qualification | _____ |
| Informal, private | _____ |
| Bible Study | _____ |
| **7. Other (Specify)** | _____ |

|  |  |
|------|-------|
| **Total (a)** | _____ |
| **Full Week (b)** | 168 |
| **Difference (a–b or b–a)** | _____ |

# Endnotes

## Introduction

1   **John Stott,** *Issues facing Christians Today* (Basingstoke: Marshall Pickering, 1984), p. 162.

2   **Leland Ryken,** *Work and Leisure in Christian Perspective* (Leicester: Inter-Varsity Press, 1989). This book includes an interesting history of man's view of work.

3   **Alistair Mackenzie** and **Wayne Kirkland,** *Where's God on Monday?* (Colorado Springs, CO: NavPress, 2003). This book deals with the wider definition of work which is not covered in my book. They also deal well with the misconceptions of dualism, i.e. 'clergy' vs 'laity' or 'secular' vs 'spiritual'.

4   **Wayne Grudem,** *Business for the Glory of God* (Wheaton, IL: Crossway, 2003), p. 13.

5   Ibid.

6   www.gg2w.org.uk

## Chapter 1

1   **Deepak Lal,** *Reviving the Invisible Hand* (Princeton University Press, 2006); **P.J. O'Rourke,** *On the Wealth of Nations* (New York: Atlantic Monthly Press, 2007).

2   Quoted by **O'Rourke,** *On the Wealth of Nations.*

3   **Leland Ryken,** *Work and Leisure in Christian Perspective* (Leicester: Inter-Varsity Press, 1989).

4   **Wayne Grudem,** *Business for the Glory of God* (Wheaton, IL: Crossway, 2003).

5   www.insurancejournal.com/news/west/2006/09/06/72065.htm

6   For example, **Brian Edwards,** *The Ten Commandments* (Epson: Day One Publications, 2002) or **Philip Ryken,** *Written in Stone* (Wheaton, IL: Crossway, 2003). Both of these books apply the Ten Commandments to modern society.

7   **Deepak Lal,** *Reviving the Invisible Hand* (Princeton University Press, 2006).

8   **George Grant,** *Bringing in the Sheaves: Transforming Poverty into Productivity* (Atlanta: American Vision Press, 1985).

## Chapter 2

1   **Mark Greene,** *Thank God it's Monday* (Bletchley: Scripture Union, 2005).

2   Abraham Maslow. He has published a great deal, most of which is not relevant to this book. Readers are, therefore, referred to his website, www.maslow.com.

3   **Brian Rosner,** *Beyond Greed* (Matthias Media, 2006).

4   www.infoplease.com

5   **Mark Greene,** *Thank God it's Monday,* p. 15.

## Chapter 3

1  **D.A. Carson,** *Becoming Conversant with the Emerging Church* (Grand Rapids, MI: Zondervan, 2005).

## Chapter 4

1  **Brian Edwards,** *Little people in Paul's letters* (Leominster: Day One, 2005).

## Chapter 7

1  **Larry Burkett,** *The Word on Finances* (Chicago: Moody, 1994). Burkett's books on management and finance are very helpful. His legacy lives on in the organization which he co-founded and can be accessed on www.crown.org. It is worth consulting this web site, especially if you live in the USA. **Larry Burkett,** *Preparing for Retirement* (Chicago: Moody Press, 1992).

# About Day One:

## Day One's threefold commitment:

- To be faithful to the Bible, God's inerrant, infallible Word;
- To be relevant to our modern generation;
- To be excellent in our publication standards.

*I continue to be thankful for the publications of Day One. They are biblical; they have sound theology; and they are relative to the issues at hand. The material is condensed and manageable while, at the same time, being complete—a challenging balance to find. We are happy in our ministry to make use of these excellent publications.*

**JOHN MACARTHUR, PASTOR-TEACHER, GRACE COMMUNITY CHURCH, CALIFORNIA**

*It is a great encouragement to see Day One making such excellent progress. Their publications are always biblical, accessible and attractively produced, with no compromise on quality. Long may their progress continue and increase!*

**JOHN BLANCHARD, AUTHOR, EVANGELIST AND APOLOGIST**

Visit our web site for more information and to request a free catalogue of our books.

**www.dayone.co.uk**

## Genesis for today

ANDY MCINTOSH

208 PAGES PAPERBACK

978–1–903087–15–2

Andy McIntosh is a scientist who sees no contradiction between the science he writes and lectures about, and the events of creation described in the book of Genesis. He believes that all Christian doctrine, directly or indirectly, is founded in the literal events of the first eleven chapters of the Bible, and that these 'foundations' of the faith have been undermined in the church by the fallible theories of evolution.

A valuable addition to the Creation versus Evolution debate.

Andy McIntosh, DSc, FIMA, CMath, FEI, CEng, FInstP, MIGEM, FRAeS is Professor of Thermodynamics and Combustion Theory at the University of Leeds. He has had a career spanning thirty years of conducting scientific research in mathematics, combustion and aeronautics both in academia and government establishments. He is married with three children and speaks regularly both in the UK and abroad concerning the importance of origins. Latterly, his research has brought in the life sciences with the study of the bombardier beetle, and the whole field of biomimetics—learning engineering solutions from nature.

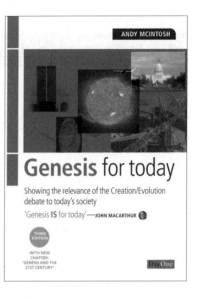

**'This is an excellent book for all to read and to give as a gift to interested sceptics.'**
*EVANGELICAL TIMES*

**'For those who have eyes to see, here is ample proof that God's revealed truth is as trustworthy as ever—and infinitely more certain than every human speculation.'**
*JOHN MACARTHUR*

**He made the stars also:**
**What the Bible says about the stars**

STUART BURGESS

192PP, ILLUSTRATED PAPERBACK

ISBN 978–1–903087–13–8

He made
the stars also
What the Bible says about the stars

**Stuart Burgess**          DayOne

This book teaches clearly and biblically the purpose of the stars and the question of extra-terrestrial life. Dr Burgess explains how the earth has a unique purpose in supporting life and how the stars have a singular purpose in shining light on it. He explains why the universe contains such natural beauty and how the stars reveal God's character.

Dr Stuart Burgess is Head of Department of Mechanical Engineering at the University of Bristol. His research areas include the study of design in nature. He previously worked in industry, designing rocket and satellite systems for the European Space Agency. He is winner of the Worshipful Company of Turners Gold Medal for the design of the solar array deployment system on the £1·4 billion ENVISAT earth observation satellite.

'Dr Burgess has a very clear style and his book brims with interesting material. It will be greatly appreciated.'
—*DR PETER MASTERS, METROPOLITAN TABERNACLE*

## Truth, lies and science education

PAUL TAYLOR

160PP, ILLUSTRATED PAPERBACK

ISBN 978–1–84625–071–2

Most of us are totally unaware of what actually goes on in the teaching environment in the classroom. We may attend parents' evenings and discuss with the teacher the progress of our children in the classroom. We help with (and sometimes actually do) our children's homework. Parents and grandparents will talk with their children and grandchildren about what they are taught, but the children are unable to explain why they are taught what they are taught or what are the philosophical ideologies behind the teaching. In this carefully researched book, Paul Taylor powerfully and devastatingly brings to light the underlying thinking that is the basis for so much of what is taught in our modern schools.

I can warmly commend this book to everyone that has an interest in the education of our young people.
DR A J MONTY WHITE,
CHIEF EXECUTIVE, ANSWERS IN GENESIS

Students spend more time with their teachers/professors than they do with their parents in learning to understand what life is all about. As a result, their formalized education has a great impact on their worldview. Truth, Lies and Science Education is a valiant attempt to tackle this issue head on to engage the education system and parents in understanding the realities of what is being taught to children and how they are being conformed to a secular way of thinking about every aspect of reality.
KEN HAM,
PRESIDENT OF ANSWERS IN GENESIS, USA

## God's prescription for a healthy marriage

ANDREW OLIVER

160PP, ILLUSTRATED PAPERBACK

ISBN 978–1–84625–095–8

The family is under threat. Contemporary culture and changes in legislation are seeking to redefine its structure, parents are increasingly giving over to the state the responsibility of disciplining their children, and homes are constantly bombarded by immoral images of the 'family' through TV. The great need today is to return to biblical principles for family life. The Bible is God's manual for the people he created in his image, and therefore it has much to say on this crucial issue. Here, Andy Oliver guides us helpfully through the biblical teaching on marriage and family life, and emphasizes the need to follow God's Word if we are to build solid foundations for a healthy family.

Andy Oliver comes from Northern Ireland, where he ran his own small business before entering full-time Christian ministry. He is engaged in missionary service and pastoral ministry in Albania, and he is a frequent speaker at university student meetings on behalf of BSKSH (IFES Albania). He and his wife, Ela, have two daughters, Rakela and Emma, and a son, Jack.

Across Europe, and, indeed, the Western world, the crisis in marriage and family life is impacting Christian and non-Christian alike, and Andy Oliver's book provides a timely reminder of God's good purposes for us. His approach is thought-provoking and uncompromising and, while you might not agree with every application, you will benefit greatly from this refreshingly direct and practical introduction to what the Bible teaches.

JONATHAN LAMB, AUTHOR, DIRECTOR OF LANGHAM PREACHING (LANGHAM PARTNERSHIP INTERNATIONAL) AND FORMER ASSOCIATE GENERAL SECRETARY OF IFES